What readers have said …

Invisible Giants is a generous offering, deeply personal and beautifully written in clear, engaging prose. It demonstrates, rather than simply explains, why Leaders' Quest has transformed the personal and work lives of the individuals who have joined these journeys.

Tom Glocer, former CEO of Thomson Reuters

An important and enjoyable read for business leaders who want to better understand the complex relationships between people, culture, attitudes and opportunities that shape our world. Invisible Giants challenges us to think differently about business and the role of leaders. Reading it is, in itself, an inspiring journey, with wonderful stories of exceptional people beating the odds to accomplish extraordinary things.

Bob Bechek, Worldwide Managing Director, Bain & Company

Many have written about leadership. Invisible Giants explores its moral meaning. How can we connect with what really matters and find an inner voice that changes the way we see our work? Lindsay Levin's organisation leads transformative personal experiences and she writes beautifully about success – and failure. She seeks inspiration from grassroots leaders, and takes people to worlds they never normally encounter. Seeing this awaken leadership potential is incredibly exciting.

Koy Thomson, Chief Executive, Children in Crisis

Every corporate leader who yearns to redefine the role of business-beyond-profit should read Invisible Giants. Lindsay's quest takes us to Indian slums and South African prisons, but most importantly on a transformative inner journey – one which starts with curiosity, grows into compassion and leads to courageous actions, changing the world one leader at a time.

Virginie Helias, Global Director, Sustainability, Procter & Gamble

Invisible Giants is truly inspiring. Lindsay Levin's work takes her to places where committed people are transforming lives. It's not about privileged do-gooders who clamour for media attention, but about "karmayogis": people who bring about change in quiet and purposeful ways. It contains powerful lessons for everyone, including business leaders, who, says Lindsay, can learn to put social purpose at the heart of company identity.

Anu Aga, Chairperson, Teach For India; Director, Thermax Limited; Member of Parliament, India

Invisible Giants is an extraordinary, warts-and-all account of an evolving cultural revolution designed to jump leaders into 21st century realities.

John Elkington, Executive Chairman, Volans Ventures; Co-founder of Environmental Data Services (ENDS) and SustainAbility

Invisible Giants

~ Changing the world one step at a time ~

Lindsay Levin

 Vala

First published in 2013 by Vala Publishing Co-operative

Copyright © Lindsay Levin

Vala Publishing Co-operative Ltd

8 Gladstone Street, Bristol, BS3 3AY, UK

For further information on Vala publications, see

www.valapublishers.coop or write to info@valapublishers.coop

Cover design by Sue Gent

www.lupercaliadesign.co.uk

Typography by Michaela Meadow

www.michaelameadow.com

Typeset in Freya, designed by Saku Heinänen

Printed and bound by CPI Antony Rowe, Chippenham, UK

The paper used is Munken, which is FSC certified.

All the author's royalties from the sale of this book will go to the

Leaders' Quest Foundation, a charity registered in the UK, the US and India.

www.leadersquest.org

A CIP catalogue record for this title is available from

the British Library.

ISBN 978-1-908363-05-3

For Mum and Dad

and

for Naidu

All know that the drop merges into the ocean,
but few know that the ocean merges into the drop.

~ Kabir

Contents

Introduction
What Really Matters?

"Remember when you were in school?" asked the CEO from Chicago. "And there was this really nerdy kid, with no friends, and everyone – you included – made fun of him?"

It was the last night of a busy week in China. I was accompanying a group of leaders, from diverse backgrounds and countries, who had travelled with me to Beijing and Sichuan Province. We were here to explore China's culture, to meet people from different walks of life, and to think about our own leadership roles. Like many in the group, the man from Chicago had started out feeling suspicious and rather fearful of the Chinese and their rapidly changing landscape. But now, as we sat together over dinner, reflecting on what we'd seen and heard, he had some new perspectives.

He'd spent six days meeting the bosses of big businesses, professors of geopolitics and internet entrepreneurs. He'd toured a factory where twenty thousand workers made shoes, eaten lunch in a canteen which served four thousand in a single sitting, then met with managers to discuss supply chains and dwindling profit margins. He'd watched children fly kites and couples dance the tango in the morning light of a Beijing park, then taken the metro to one of China's most respected universities, to talk with students about their dreams for the future. He'd even spent the night in a remote, northern village, where he'd shared a two-room house with three colleagues, a farmer and his family, in temperatures that reached minus fifteen degrees.

And at some point during the week, a small encounter, or perhaps a chance accumulation of them, had awakened in him a new appreciation of who he was and how he was connected to everyone around him. It was a subtle shift, a magical moment. Something had clicked into place and he'd seen the world afresh.

"I feel like, this week in China, I got to sit down and have lunch with that nerdy, ostracised kid from my classroom," he said. "I got to know him and I started to understand him. I learned who he is and why he behaves the way he does, and I discovered I could relate to him. I found that I even liked him. I'm going home tomorrow with a lot more compassion in my bones."

~

This is a book about leadership and choices in life. It's about some of the people I've met throughout the course of my work, each of whom is a leader, though not always in a conventional sense. These are the invisible giants of my story – people who emerge to lead in the most vulnerable situations, inspiring energy and confidence in those around them. They are leaders who battle against adversity, who overcome the disadvantages of a poor or non-existent education and a lack of material resources. They are female activists in marginalised communities, who campaign to end domestic violence and the exclusion of girls from school. They are business executives who choose the uphill task of trying to embed social accountability into their companies, one step at a time, despite resistance. And finally, they are the people you and I meet every day, who are changing the world in their own way, through the choices they make in their lives. This is a book about the ability, deep within all of us, to make our voices heard.

My travels over the past ten years have taken me all over the world to villages and cities, townships and slums, to meet people in all kinds of circumstances, with different points of view. I've spent time with entrepreneurs and activists, and with ordinary citizens from all social strata. Men, women and children with aspirations, energy and passion – and sometimes people worn down to a fragment of the person they wanted to be.

Many of these people have overcome obstacles, and often their own frailties, to step up and change their lives and the lives of those around them. They have struck a chord with me, not because they are inherently more virtuous than the many "visible" leaders who strive to contribute to a happier, healthier world, but because their stories are rarely told and because they have a vital role to play in creating a brighter future.

I've been on a journey of surprises, of deep sadness, and of great joy. We might debate whether the cup of life is half empty or half full, yet in my experience it is overflowing with the infinite potential of people to grow and to create. Today, despite the evident challenges facing all of us, I find myself full of hope. I have written this book to try and share some of this optimism.

~

In 2001, I founded a social enterprise called Leaders' Quest. My goal was to inspire people to ask tough questions about life and the way they (and I) choose to live it, and to look for answers together. I joined forces with two friends, Sue Cheshire and Gene Early, and we came up with the core idea of a "Quest", the essence of which is the search for insight and a larger sense of individual, and collective, purpose. The concept has evolved over the intervening years, yet today it remains remarkably true to the original idea.

A Quest brings together a group of leaders from all kinds of backgrounds: directors of multinational companies, self-made entrepreneurs and heads of non-profit organisations, as well as teachers, government leaders and artists. It takes us to many interesting parts of the world: India, China, Brazil, Argentina, South Africa, Mozambique, Nigeria, Kenya, Turkey, Russia, the US and the UK – the list is growing. It offers a rich choice of visits and reflections, packed into a week spent exploring business, civil society and government. It's an intense journey of immersion, during which we get to know the country and its culture, meet with a wide range of people, and think about who we are and the opportunities we have been given.

Every Quest is unique and deliberately filled with contrasting experiences. A day in Hyderabad might begin at one of the finest technology parks in the world, meeting with CEOs and the young engineers they have hired to design future products. It might end a mile away in an informal settlement where people will sacrifice almost anything for a job, the chance to be needed and to play a part in their own vibrant ecosystem. We might visit a housing project in Rio, sit under a tree and talk with villagers outside Maputo, or exchange ideas with students in Lagos. In Guangzhou we might get up at dawn to cycle through the city as it wakes. Then head out to a factory making toys for European, American and Chinese consumers, tour the production line, then visit dormitories provided for the young migrant workers who have come from all over the country to work here.

At the end of a Quest, it's important that we leave behind something that will really benefit the people who have been kind enough to spend time with us. Some of these hosts are part of the establishment, informal or otherwise, while others come from the poorest communities. They all take pride in talking about their lives and what they are doing to change them, and more often than not, they ask us to return. Crucially, over the last decade, they have helped to create a powerful global community – a network of people with a shared interest in making a positive contribution. Many of those who participate – both hosts and the people who come with us – go on to form new partnerships across continents and sectors, creating innovative products (banking services for the unbanked in Africa, a distribution network for Indian-made electric cars in the UK) and community initiatives (free counselling centres for Chinese migrant workers, computer labs in Mumbai slums).

Underpinning all this is the belief that the most powerful learning in life typically comes through experience, rather than teaching or debate. We want to bring people together to learn from the unfamiliar and to recognise the capacity they have – whoever they are – to improve the world around them. We want to help leaders understand the contrasts and connections, both visible and invisible, between people everywhere. Ultimately, a Quest is all about personal choice and discovering what makes life meaningful.

~

More than ten years ago, our pilot Quest took place in Silicon Valley, where we delved deep into the world of innovation and entrepreneurship. By the time I got home to London, I knew there was no turning back. I would quit the CEO role I held at the time, and focus exclusively on creating a new enterprise dedicated to helping leaders grow. What might have been a lonely path turned into a shared endeavour, when I was joined by Fields Wicker-Miurin to help build Leaders' Quest. Other people followed, each with their own special contribution.

The early days saw us travelling to some of the emerging markets at the leading edge of change – countries of startling contrast and extremes, which are home to many of humanity's greatest challenges and opportunities. Together, we designed and led Quests in powerhouse economies like India, China and Brazil, and nations in the midst of other kinds of transformation, like South Africa and Mozambique. We went to São Paulo and Johannesburg where the consequences of urban poverty and limited access to healthcare and education are clear to see. We navigated Mumbai and Lagos, seriously polluted cities with crumbling or non-existent infrastructure, rife with corruption, both hidden and blatant, into which hundreds of thousands of new migrants flood every year in search of work. At the same time, we discovered the positives that these places have to share: enterprise and creativity, spiritual and intellectual energy, and rich cultural heritage. At worst, extreme circumstances leave people in a state of hopelessness; at best they elicit transformational courage and leadership. This is what we wanted to explore.

Our work struck a chord. Soon we were running multiple programmes every year, from intensive two-day Quests for the global leadership teams of multinational firms, to week-long "deep dives" for fifteen individuals, intent on defining new priorities for themselves.

Over the years Leaders' Quest has begun to work with organisations as well as the individuals who lead them. Some of these people are searching for new solutions and trying to foster trust and inclusiveness in their companies and institutions. Some have come to realise that a narrow focus on profit is not enough, and that without a deeper sense of accountability to the communities in which they work, they will find themselves without the legitimacy to operate. We believe that businesses can choose to play a far larger role in mitigating some of the negative consequences of economic growth and in shaping the future constructively. In effect, they can learn how to put social purpose at the heart of company identity – not instead of profit, but alongside it.

Beneath the surface, we have consistently found that people are looking for greater meaning in their lives. For some, fresh experiences reveal something vital that they didn't know was missing. There are the NGO leaders, determined to change society through persuasion or coercion, who are often surprised to learn how much they share with those they consider adversaries. There are the company leaders who want to better understand the world in order to win, but who discover, along the way, that how they run the race is as important as the destination. Or, who summon the authenticity to go against the tide, despite uncertainty and personal risk. There are people questioning whether spending the first half of their lives taking everything, only to wake up some time later with a desire to give something back, is really a good enough way to live.

Leaders' Quest began as a response to the part of me that was full of hope for the world, but also overwhelmed by the suffering and inequality that marked so many lives. It stemmed from my belief in the capacity of people to dream a better future, and then make it happen, and my feeling that people are increasingly searching for a bolder, more imaginative response. It also came from my fear that many of us, me included, were heading in the wrong direction, and had somehow lost the connection between head and soul – something that I felt, instinctively, was lurking just beneath the skin for many of the people I met.

I started out with some unanswered questions of my own – questions about healing, fairness and the human spirit – none of them original, but for me they were new.

Today, I think I am closer to understanding some of the answers. I've spent time between extremes, with people fighting hard to preserve the status quo and those struggling to break it. I've been struck by the relationship between the fundamental drive to live a worthwhile life and the capacity of people to endure and survive when they have to – what the writer and Holocaust survivor Viktor Frankl describes as "the will to meaning".[1] I've been inspired by the awesome potential within every individual, if only we can find more ways to liberate it. I'm left with a profound feeling of optimism and a sense of the possible, born of seeking to embrace, rather than hide from, the things in life that are difficult or painful.

Invisible Giants is a book about being, as much as doing. It's about my own quest, among extraordinary leaders in unlikely places, to ask "what really matters?" and to find out where the answers can take me.

Chapter One
Building Bridges

S everal synchronous things happened at the start of 2001 to prompt a change of course in my life, and one of them arrived in an envelope from Oxfam. My husband, David, and I had been active supporters for several years and just as the idea of Leaders' Quest was taking shape, the charity invited us to visit some of its work in Ethiopia. We knew at once that we wanted to go. We both shared an interest in development and a desire to know more about the practicalities of making it work on the ground. The continent of Africa also had a particular draw for David. He'd arrived in Britain as a small child, the son of political refugees fleeing the white ruling party in Rhodesia, and I think he always regretted the lost opportunity to grow up there, even more so when his father died a few years later, leaving a teenage son who felt somehow severed from his own roots.

When the time came for the two of us to set off for Addis Ababa a few weeks later, our leave-taking was unexpectedly traumatic. We'd arranged to leave our three sons (then seven, five and turning two), in the care of David's mother, Leah. On the day of our departure we pulled up outside her home, our car loaded with suitcases, boxes of Lego and favourite soft toys, with the boys bouncing excitedly on the back seat.

Once inside the flat, however, our eldest son, Zac, grew increasingly anxious. He began to panic and then burst into tears. Between sobs he told us that he knew our plane was going to crash and that he'd never see us again. There had been a recent headline air disaster, and in his young mind, this was the way flights ended. Zac clung to us for dear life, inconsolable. Nothing we could say made the least bit of difference. The clock ticked on. We had to leave or we'd miss the flight. Agonisingly, we prised ourselves from his arms, leaving Leah clutching Zac, who was sobbing and raging as we fled. The door of the flat slammed shut behind us and the wailing grew faint as we ran down the road, full of guilt. We sat silent and glum all the way to the airport and didn't fully recover until we called home after landing in Addis Ababa. All was well, Leah told us. Zac had staged a robust and rapid recovery, aided by her homemade chicken stew and ice cream.

The first night in Addis felt magical. We were staying in a somewhat frayed but perfectly adequate hotel, home to the occasional business traveller, along with aid workers and UN delegates. Most of them were there in a variety of roles, to help address the long list of woes – from food crises to a chronic shortage of healthcare –with which the country had to contend. After an early dinner, David and I set off to explore the local neighbourhood. It felt more like an extended village than a city, with homes spilling out onto the streets and people going about their evening business in the open, cooking, washing, or sitting and talking at the side of the road. A little girl, barefoot and dressed in a dirty red dress, took us under her wing. She had wide, excited eyes and a playful laugh, and she chatted constantly in her native tongue while she darted in and out of ramshackle huts and houses, leaping out to surprise us every few minutes as she tracked our progress through the streets.

We turned a corner and came upon a wide open space that served as a sports field. Around the perimeter was a poorly kept running track, and to one side, a bank of broad, stone terrace steps – spectator seating, I presumed. There, in the light of the moon and the stars, a couple of dozen athletes were at work, running circuits on the track, sprinting in short bursts, skipping rope, then pounding their way through hundreds of step ups and push ups. We sat for a long time on the terraces, watching young men and women as they pushed themselves to new limits, all part of a sundown-community of aspiration. I felt very happy to be there, far away from the familiarity of my daily life for a few days, to absorb the buzz of energy in the hot night air of this ancient, intriguing land.

The following morning, we ate breakfast early with the small group of fellow travellers with whom we were to spend the week, then helped load up two Jeeps with rucksacks and supplies, ready to set off on a day-long drive to the Yejju Wadla Delanta plateau. It was a stunning, bone-jarring journey. As Addis petered out into a series of scattered hamlets, we began to climb. We followed the twists and turns of mountain passes, dropping occasionally to cross a rock-strewn valley or to bump our way, painfully slowly, across a broad, dry river bed, lined with smooth, pale stones. From time to time, we pulled up at the side of the road to stretch our legs and look out over wave upon wave of blue-grey mountains under a clear and fathomless sky.

The plateau, when we reached it, was exquisite in a bare and rugged way. It was home to around a quarter of a million people, all of them survivors of the cyclical bouts of drought and starvation that had long plagued the region. We stayed there for several nights, with Oxfam's local team, in a simple house that served as office and sleeping quarters, and went out with them each morning to meet the people they were there to serve, and learn about their work.

One day stands out, drained of colour, with everything turned to shades of grey and sepia by the relentless sun and the fragility of life on the plateau. Once a month, Oxfam opened its local warehouse, to distribute grain to rural families who would come from twenty miles around or more, travelling mainly on foot or the occasional donkey, to collect their quota. Without this food source, people would starve to death. We had spent the previous day learning about the efforts of families to improve yields in some of the most inhospitable, deforested territory in Africa. We stopped for a while to join in play with some of the ragged children who gathered on the open ground at the edge of scant settlements to pass time, and exchanged shy smiles with others who stood watch over the occasional lean cow, swatting at the clouds of flies that buzzed around them. We spoke with people as they tended precious single blades of green wheat in the burnt earth, and witnessed their painstaking efforts to improve irrigation, channelling water into small hand-crafted gullies. These were families teetering on the edge of existence, with nowhere else to go.

There was palpable tension in the air as the hour of the hand-out approached. Skinny guards with big sticks kept people back from the warehouse as a large, glass-eyed and listless crowd gathered, a stream of humanity descending from the surrounding hills. Most were men, old beyond their years. I imagined that all of them yearned to be able to support their families, to earn a living and sustain themselves. But, with year after year of needing help just to stay alive, they seemed to have grown worn and sapped of hope.

That evening we talked late into the night with Oxfam's staff – all of them Ethiopian – who were haunted by the fear that their efforts weren't enough, that they needed to do more, and do better. There were no easy answers. I lay awake into the early hours and thought about the resourcefulness that comes from working at the edge, and how doing this requires courage and patience, in ways that an easier path through life does not. The over-riding feeling I had then, and have often had since, was one of profound gratitude for the men and women who emerge to lead in such difficult circumstances. I lay there looking up at the stars, some faint, others bright, and I thought about the dignity of countless, committed invisible giants, the world over. I thought about potential, and what was lost through apathy or lack of self-belief.

The following day, we left the haunting beauty of Delanta and made the long, rugged drive back to Addis to spend a couple of days meeting some of the local organisations which were working with the urban poor. There, on the edge of a slum, I met a young, rather beautiful woman, who lived in a shack about eight feet square, made of random bits of wood, corrugated iron and cardboard. She sat outside her home making injera, the traditional Ethiopian flat bread, to sell to the occasional passer-by. Beside her on the ground, immobile and wrapped loosely in a blanket, lay a small child. The woman and I exchanged smiles and nods of encouragement and then she stood up and beckoned me inside. The room was very dark after the stark, bright sunlight outside. I noticed the walls were lined with old newspapers and the dirt floor was swept clean, save for a pile of clothes and a couple of folded rugs in the corner. There was no furniture. We stood together for a while, surveying her home, and then stepped back outside. With the help of our interpreter, I asked if we could sit and talk. The woman nodded yes and we sat down on the earth, beside the pot she used for cooking.

Her name, she said, was Hasiya. She was the mother of two, her first child a healthy son of eight, and her second, a daughter, born with cerebral palsy four years earlier. When the girl was born, her husband told her he couldn't cope and so, he left. Hasiya hadn't seen him since. Her son was at school, though it was a struggle to pay for his uniform and books. We spoke about the exorbitant rent she paid for her shack to the local landlord – all part of a stark, raw state of day-to-day existence.

Hasiya's situation felt to me like the absolute certainty of uncertainty, a deep and apparently unbreakable cycle of poverty. I found myself struggling to hold back the tears that come when there are no words, looking at her, one mother to another, with a heavy sense of inadequacy. I thought of my own children and our wrenching departure some ten days earlier. Here I was, looking into the face of a young mother with whom I shared so much more than either of us could fully comprehend. Yet she would never have the opportunities that I had, and we both knew it. I sat looking at the woman and her little girl and as I did so, I felt something move inside me. If there was a single moment that fixed the core of Leaders' Quest, then this was it: a sense of recognition, to be repeated many times in the years to come, and the knowledge that she and I were part of the same whole. There was shame too, because of the gap between us. And a kind of acceptance that this was the beautiful, sometimes cruel world that I was part of, and the way I chose to be in it would give my life meaning.

~

Ethiopia was a gift and I came home ready to build something new. Fifteen years into a successful business career, I'd grown increasingly restless, fuelled by an old disquiet and a feeling that there was something different I had to do if only I could figure it out.

From university, I'd joined the strategy consulting firm Bain and Company, where I'd spent a formative couple of years before changing tack to join my father's business in the motor trade in southeast England. By the time I reached my late twenties, I'd become the CEO of a chain of car dealerships, service centres and crash repair shops. It had proved a steep learning curve. Shortly after I joined the business, we'd come close to bankruptcy. We'd had to haul ourselves back from the edge over many months, driven, in my case, by sheer hard work and a fear of failure. Slowly, we moved the business onto a surer track. As we did so, I came to understand that my real passion was people. I loved building teams and I wanted to create a great place to work where everyone was motivated and energised. Ours was a service business: it mattered that we cared about our customers. And as far as I could see, the only way we'd be successful was if we also cared about our co-workers. When I thought about the company and the people in it, I didn't see separate teams and functions, divided into silos. I saw a web of relationships within the business and beyond, shaped by what we did rather than what we said. I saw how stress in one place had unintended knock-on effects elsewhere; the frequent disconnect between what one person says and another one hears.

The culture of our company changed and people outside increasingly took notice. We won a string of awards and I began to receive invitations to speak on leadership at events around the country. As I did so, I found myself looking for inspiration from other fields – particularly amongst NGOs working in global development, an interest sparked by travel and curiosity about different cultures. My relationships grew more and more eclectic. My friends included social entrepreneurs and activists, all of them intent, in various ways, on challenging the status quo. I was intrigued by the seams that run between contrasting ways of looking at things. Few of my colleagues in business were interested in, or knowledgeable about, the development sector. Most of them assumed that the people in it were idealistic, ineffective and generally "anti" enterprise. The NGO people I knew, on the other hand, were often equally dismissive and judgemental of business as being selfish and self-serving, lacking in morality, with an overly simplistic and greedy view of what was, in fact, a complex world.

This apparently binary divide disturbed me. I recognised a pattern of rushing to conclusions to support assumptions about who was right and wrong and how everything ought to be. I saw it in others and I saw it in myself. Life seemed to be made up of opposing camps determined to fight one another, when in fact we could, and should, be working together. I hated the mistrust, and my instinct in the face of it was to try to build a bridge.

As I looked about me in search of a new direction, I had the idea that if I could bring people together from different, even conflicting perspectives, on neutral ground and into each other's lives, we would all see ourselves in a new light and be changed by the experience. I turned to my two friends, Sue Cheshire and Gene Early, both of whom were struggling with some of the same questions. Together, the three of us began to figure out what role we might play in responding to some of the challenges we saw around us. Sue and I agreed to take a few days out from our day jobs to visit Gene and his wife, Benedicte, at their home in Silicon Valley. I had no idea just how pivotal the trip would be. Gene put together an intense schedule of meetings with entrepreneurs and innovators from different fields and by the end of our time together, the idea of Leaders' Quest had fully crystallised. We committed ourselves to designing a five-day trip to California and inviting a group of leaders to come with us the following spring, to experience some of the best of the inspiration and energy to be found there. The trip would comprise visits chosen for their mutual benefit to visitors and hosts. Although I never imagined it at the time, it would prove to be the first step in creating a powerful global community – a network of people with a shared interest in making a positive contribution to their surroundings, whatever the field they worked in.

Beginning a new venture alongside an existing CEO position meant the work had to be slotted into late nights and weekends. But right from the start, I knew I was going to find a way to leave my existing role and turn my new one into a full-time responsibility. Towards the end of our stay in San Francisco, I was already planning what would follow – our first programme in India would take place the next year.

~

Steadily, Leaders' Quest took off. We added new ideas and destinations every year: South Africa and Mozambique, China, then Brazil, Kenya, Russia and Turkey. We regularly found ourselves welcomed into homes, health clinics, businesses and community centres. To begin with, this generosity took me by surprise, but it was to become one of the great pleasures associated with our work. People are curious about one another. They want to be generous to those who have come from half a world away. They want to share their stories and, often, they have a lot to say.

Sometimes the circumstances were extreme, and the lessons poignant.

There was the time we walked into a huge and shabby tent full of homeless people in the middle of Old Delhi on a sharp, cold winter's night. I was with my good friend Sanjay, leader of the city's largest outreach programme for the homeless, and a small group of visitors, all of them part of a Quest in India. The canvas tent, held down with guy ropes and rusty iron pegs, was situated on a large patch of wasteland beside a cemetery, just off one of Delhi's main roads. Inside it, were some five hundred men and boys, all of them camped for the night on packed lines of bamboo beds that snaked up and down. Men sat, four or five to a bed, wrapped in grey blankets, whilst others slept in dense rows, dead to the noise around them. Boys played games in cramped corners or stared vacantly in front of them, tired, or high on alcohol or drugs. Old men gathered a little apart, each in their own dignified space in spite of the press of bodies around them. The air was stale and warm with an acrid taste that caught in the back of the throat.

Our group fell quiet at first, shocked, recalibrating and taking stock. People of all ages began to crowd around us, eager to break the monotony of another transient night. They shuffled up to make space and invited us to sit beside them on their beds. I did so, and then beckoned the little group of visitors to do the same. Some hesitated for a few seconds, taken aback at what they'd stepped into. Several people had picked up stomach bugs from the food they had eaten in India and I knew they were appalled to witness, for the first time, the filthy living conditions of people who had no place to wash, no access to sanitation, and lacked even a change of clothes. But gradually a peace seemed to come into the tent. The heat and the fug of the space grew familiar and people began to find their voices again.

"How do you earn your living?" a Frenchman asked the crowd.

There was a teenage boy sitting cross-legged next to me, his hair in stiff and matted knots and his eyes a little too bright. He was dressed in a stained shirt and ragged trousers cut below the knee. He had no shoes and the soles of his feet were coarse and black. He'd left his home in the state of Bihar a long time back, he told us, and now he worked in the catering industry, serving food. He did a decent trade during the wedding season, but no, it was not enough to afford him a roof over his head.

Someone asked how many of them worked each day and a mass of hands shot up. It seemed everyone did, in some form or another, no matter how informal. A German woman asked about the toilet facilities.

"There's a small river that flows at the back of this place," came the reply.

"No I mean toilets! What about toilets?" she asked again.

Embarrassed, Sanjay waved his hand in the general direction of the river. "There aren't any," he said. "We manage."

There was a pause. The catering industry seemed a good track to pursue.

"How many of you work in catering?" asked the Frenchman.

Again a show of hands, more than half the crowd, it seemed. The woman sitting next to me had been struggling with the effects of "Delhi belly" for the past couple of days. Her mouth fell open, aghast, and she pulled at my sleeve.

"These boys are cooks and they have no place to wash," she said to me under her breath, her eyes shining. "I can't believe it."

In that moment, the relationship between farmer, market stall, kitchen and dining table, took on a whole new meaning. We were men, women and children who shared the same dirt, breathed the same air, whether we liked it or not. We were all part of an invisible web connecting people everywhere. A web which seemed to say: "I am part of you and you are part of me. And, yes, it's complicated."

There was silence for a while as everyone soaked up what it meant to simply be present with one another.

Then someone mentioned finance, a subject on which many of us, as visitors, were brimming with sophisticated expertise. A couple of years previously, Sanjay and the shelter volunteers had fought and won the right for homeless people to hold bank accounts, despite their lack of status or permanent address. Here, and in other shelters across the city, men and women of every age came each night to queue for the right to hand over a few rupees from their earnings, and to put them into a savings account and Sanjay wanted to show us how the system worked. We squeezed our way through the crowd to the far end of the tent, where a steady stream of people arrived to use the mobile banking service. We watched as a young woman, slightly built and wrapped in a shawl, arrived at the head of the line and handed over her bank card to be swiped ceremoniously through a small handheld wireless device by the man in charge. Slowly, she pressed her forefinger onto the machine's pad so that her print could be scanned for identification. She was saving, she told us, to build for her future.

Here was technology giving birth in some modest way to identity. The bank card, with a photograph and a finger print that said: "I am somebody." Sanjay stood looking on, close to bursting with pride and delight.

"If this man dies tomorrow on the street," he announced loudly and excitedly, pointing to an elderly gentleman who was standing in the queue, clutching his coveted bank card to his skinny ribs and nodding proudly. "If this man dies tomorrow, then they will find his card! They will know who he is! He will have a name and they will know where he comes from. He can have a burial. He exists!"

This was to become a familiar moment for me. Here we were, seeing something as ordinary as a bank card in a completely new light. It was a piece of plastic that stood for identity, equality, and basic human rights. It had the capacity to acknowledge, far beyond the simple service on offer. I thought about the power of technology to make a difference in ordinary lives, when thoughtfully applied. It called for imagination and another way of seeing. It required co-operation and perseverance from people like Sanjay, but also from others on the inside – in this case software developers, bankers, government officials. Those with the capacity, if they chose to use it, to gather people into humanity's collective tent, instead of leaving them outside.

~

As interest grew in what we had to offer, so did the need to build a team. Gene continued to play an important role, but was still heavily committed to his work in California, where he was a founding member of a genetics company. It would be a few years before he made the decision to join us as a partner. Sue also had another full-time role. Whilst she remained an enthusiastic and encouraging friend to our new venture, she was not ready to make a shift and join me in taking it forward. I therefore found myself alone, with a big idea that I knew

I had to develop. If I had to do it solo, so be it, but what I really wanted was to find an initial partner, and then many others, to do it with me.

At the end of 2001, as I began to invite people to join the first India Quest, David came home one night and said, "I've just had dinner with a friend who you need to meet. Don't be put off by the impressive CV or the long name – she's great."

A few weeks later I found myself having tea in the unlikely surroundings of the Athenaeum Club in Piccadilly, London with Fields Wicker-Miurin. Born in North Carolina to academic parents, Fields had left home and moved to Europe at the age of seventeen. Much later, she married an Italian economist and central banker, Paolo, and picked up the Miurin in her name. By the time we met, Fields had already enjoyed a flourishing career in business, finance and government and received a formidable education along the way. She too was trying to figure out what kind of contribution she could make in the next chapter of her life. Fields joined the India Quest as a participant, and a couple of months later, in a coffee shop in Pimlico, we agreed to become partners. She brought with her a new sense of aspiration and professionalism. She had bigger dreams for us than I did and was patient enough to let me figure it out. All the same, she was horrified when, on our first trip together to prepare for a Quest, I mislaid my passport three times in the space of half an hour and emptied out the contents of my handbag on the airport floor. She smiled encouragingly and did her best to look calm.

"I thought God what have I done!" Fields told me later over a glass of wine. "How the hell does this woman make it round the world?"

Other people joined us: Diane Richards and Alison Daly to design and support programmes; Jason Brooks who introduced us to a China we would never have met on our own; new partners Kenzie Kwong and Melanie Katzman from Hong Kong and New York, who made an instinctive decision to give up significant parts of their lives and take up the challenge of developing an idea they believed in.

Implicit in each Quest were tough questions about choices and priorities – the environmental and social costs of growth, as well as the gains; the dislocation of families in an increasingly urban world; widening inequality and a lack of access to basic services for large swathes of society. We were soon being asked to design Quests for government leaders, company boards and networks of business people – and as we did so, we found ourselves asking questions about the responsibility that comes with leadership, across every field of endeavour.

Amongst my own colleagues, the openness and intensity of what we did meant we saw the best and the worst of one another from very early on. I came to believe that everyone needed, in their own way, to heal some kind of wound they didn't necessarily know they had. Something in the recipe attracted people who wanted to learn, even when it was painful to do so. There were times when anger flared in one or other of us at what we were seeing. There were waves of despondency or grief at the circumstances in which so many families lived, trapped in a deep cycle of poverty. Yet at the same time we had a lot of fun. We were exploring the world together, seeking out the most enterprising people and ideas we could find. I felt we had each made a choice to learn things that are impossible to un-know: that a person whose culture and political system are different to ours has a way of perceiving the world that's just as valuable; that a mother living on a dollar a day has the same dreams for her children as we do. In a world increasingly preoccupied with scarcity, we wanted to focus on the extraordinary abundance of human potential and go out and explore some of its edges.

Chapter Two
Inspiration in Unlikely Places

reating a Quest is like assembling a giant jigsaw puzzle, and never more so than when we start out in a new country. We talk to as many people as we can, read up on history, culture and present day trends, all well before we even set foot in the place. In China for example, our focus might be on industrialisation, the transformation of the economy and the way government works. In India, it could be the growth of technology and the outsourcing of global services to local companies. In Brazil we might explore innovation, entrepreneurialism and how to conserve natural resources. At the same time, we think about the people who will eventually come with us, and what they will want to learn. Some will come to understand a new market and experience another context, others to reflect on their own leadership and the next stages of their lives. Often it's a mixture of these.

Over the course of several visits, we build networks of interesting people, look for organisations which are doing remarkable work in different fields, and explore whatever we find that is most engaging. Finally, several months later, we bring it all together in a Quest, with the goal of giving as unvarnished, diverse and inspiring a perspective as we can on a country, some of its people, and the challenges and opportunities they are wrestling with. Sometimes the issues which stand out are painful ones.

Shortly after Fields joined me as a partner, she and I set off together for Johannesburg, to prepare our first Quest in South Africa. We were there to look at a whole range of inter-dependent issues that were shaping the nation at the time – from politics, business and agriculture, to youth unemployment and the government's policy of black economic empowerment. As we spent time talking to people, it soon became evident that we couldn't give a fair reflection of the country without exploring the escalating problem of crime. The end of apartheid, and the years that followed, had seen an explosion in robbery and brutality, and the impact on society was painful to witness. The reasons were many, the symptoms widespread. Corruption, pent up expectations, broken families, a lack of education and jobs, all played a part in a crime wave that was fuelling mistrust and fear, weakening the economy, and ruining the lives of millions of people.

South Africa appeared to me to be uplifting and depressing in equal measure. Here was a country that had made an extraordinary, turbulent transition over the previous twenty years. The grace and courage with which apartheid had been brought to a close had allowed people the world over to share the nation's sense of victory and possibility. Yet the weight of expectation that followed was impossibly heavy. Large chunks of the population felt let down by persistent graft, sustained inequality and a pace of change that meant their aspirations for jobs, housing, education and decent healthcare seemed destined to remain a distant dream.

At the same time, there were many qualities and characteristics which stood out. We met people with energy, pride and determination. We found a country that was home to some of the most ambitious social entrepreneurs we had met anywhere in the world, blessed with a can-do vision and work ethic, despite the many obstacles. They were perhaps a product of the political, economic and social history of the previous fifty years, each of them imbued with a belief that the scale of challenges they faced required that they leapfrog the present. These were exactly the kind of people whose stories we wanted to share.

One of them was a man named Taddy Blecher. Three years previously, Taddy had quit his job as one of the country's highest paid actuaries and gone to work in a township, teaching maths to under-privileged kids. Within a few months, he'd found himself teaching hundreds of children every week and he was soon struck by the extraordinary progress the children made when given the right kind of focus.

"It was incredibly exciting to realise what was possible and then to think about the huge scale of opportunity," he told us. "I realised that if we could truly unleash this talent we would literally transform the country."

Taddy came up with an idea for a revolutionary, low-cost university designed for young people from disadvantaged families. CIDA City Campus, as he named it, would teach one degree only – a BA in Business Administration, designed to foster a new generation of entrepreneurs, managers and leaders from amongst the poorest people in the country. Taddy persuaded a bank to lend him an abandoned inner city building to serve as campus, recruited volunteers from Johannesburg's business community to teach classes, and got the students to take on the cooking, cleaning and maintenance. He stocked the library with out-of-print text books donated by publishing houses, and equipped the classrooms with computers gifted by software companies. For the first few months, before the computers arrived, he photocopied images of keyboards and taught the students to touch-type on sheets of paper.

The students flourished, and within a couple of years the exam results they were achieving were excellent. CIDA's graduates were soon in hot demand among major employers. The university even organised a "suit library" of smart, second-hand clothes from which students could borrow. It was important that they looked the part when they turned up for interview.

A few months after our first meeting with Taddy, we returned to see him with a group of Quest visitors. The students took us on a tour of the campus, explained the curriculum and grilled us on our own career paths. We sat with them over lunch and did our best to respond to the myriad questions they had prepared for our visit – questions to which they clearly wanted thoughtful replies. What are the most valuable lessons you've learned so far in life? What makes a great leader? Do you think your generation is doing enough to take care of the planet?

The students had their own ideas that they wanted to share. They were exploring their ambition, both for themselves and for the country.

In many cases they also had a dream to return home one day to the often impoverished villages and townships from which they came, and make a difference to the siblings and cousins they'd left behind. They seemed to share an uplifting sense of responsibility, an instinctive sense of oneness with their people.

Later, we asked Taddy how it had all begun.

"I'd decided to leave South Africa, to get away from our history and its legacy, and to start a new life," he said. "I was all packed up and ready to go to New York. I had a great job offer and I'd said my goodbyes, but somehow it just didn't feel right. The night before I was due to fly, I didn't sleep a wink. I sat up till morning, crying my eyes out and then, very early the next day, I got in my car and I went to see my mother. I said to her 'I'm not going to leave. I'm going to stay here and help change the country.' It was a very significant moment for me. I just felt inside that I didn't want to lead a little life. I had to stay and create something worthwhile."

Taddy wasn't speaking in judgement of anyone else. He was simply describing how he'd gone about making meaning in his life. He'd taken a great education and a life of plenty and found a way to turn it into something more. In the process, he'd opened up new opportunities for thousands of young people.

Another social entrepreneur whom I met on that first trip to South Africa, and who was to become a great friend, was a woman named Lesley Ann Vine. She too was working with young people, but her focus was on those who had fallen off the tracks and become involved in crime. Lesley Ann is the founder of Khulisa (the Zulu word for nurture), an organisation created to help young offenders understand themselves and the choices that got them into trouble. Khulisa's goal is to change the life course of offenders and, in the process, change the country. By 2010, its programmes were directly or indirectly affecting the lives of around a million people a year in South Africa, including offenders, their families, at-risk youths and victims of crime. Nationally, about eighty percent of those released from prison were re-offending within a year. Amongst graduates of some of Khulisa's programmes, as few as twenty percent were found to do so.

My first meeting with Lesley Ann took place at a corner booth in a neon-lit Johannesburg coffee shop. I was there to talk about what we did and why, to learn more about her work, and to see if we could include Khulisa as part of our forthcoming Quest. Lesley Ann was waiting for me when I arrived, talking fast into her mobile phone and tapping her nails on the table. She was tall, impeccably manicured, and unexpectedly glamorous.

"OK," she said, with a familiar hug and barely a word of introduction. "Let's go!"

I gulped down a mouthful of cappuccino and she steered me through the door. We were going, she told me, to Johannesburg Maximum Security Prison, otherwise known as "Sun City", the place where the lights never go out, and home to some fourteen thousand youths and men.

Twenty minutes later, we pulled up in Lesley Ann's car in front of a fenced and walled compound, topped with barbed wire. We parked up at the entrance and walked towards a large gate beneath one of several watch-towers. It was the first time I'd set foot inside a prison and I felt self-conscious and a bit on edge. The prison guards were unhurried, joking as they signed us into the visitors' book and checked our identity papers, before they led us through the outer gate, into the building and through a series of heavy doors. We followed a large officer for several hundred yards, down spotless concrete passageways, before turning a corner to walk into a room where twenty five young men, dressed in identical vivid orange jump suits, lay face up on the floor. Arms spread, eyes closed, they were in the middle of a meditation, led by a softly spoken facilitator who gently padded about, between the bodies, in socked feet. The air was warm and stale and the gentle buzz of humming and long "ohhhmms" rose up from the linoleum.

I'd heard stories of filthy, violent, over-crowded cells that housed one hundred and thirty people in a space designed for sixty, and this tranquillity was the last thing I expected. I sat down and felt my heart beat drop. I noticed a couple of small high barred windows which let in a stream of sunlight. The atmosphere felt dense with energy, concentration and calm.

We waited until the men were finished. Slowly, they began to open their eyes and stand up, stiff-limbed and reluctant to return from wherever they had escaped. Without speaking, they unpacked a stack of plastic chairs which stood against the wall and formed a rough circle of them in the middle of the room. Lesley Ann broke the silence to signal that we should all sit. She told them that I was a visitor and asked that everyone introduce themselves. The facilitator spoke first. His name, he said, was Thabo, and he'd first encountered Khulisa whilst in prison serving time for fraud. After his release he had trained as a therapist, and this now was his work. Next up, I told the men who I was, where I was from and why I'd come to visit. I talked about Leaders' Quest and described our interest in learning about Khulisa's work and the impact it was having on their lives. Then, each prisoner introduced himself in identical fashion, telling me his name, age, how long he was serving and for which crime. All of them, except one man who was wearing a woollen beanie hat. He spoke last and only after a long pause.

"My name's Mohale. I'm twenty one years old and I'm serving forty eight years …" he said, his voice trailing to a standstill as he lowered his head and looked at the floor. He didn't say why he was there.

I did the maths in my head. All told, a total of four hundred and twenty eight years to serve, ages between seventeen and twenty two, two white men and twenty three black men. There were two murderers, eighteen armed robbers, four rapists and Mohale, with his crime without words.

We began to talk. I was particularly struck by one of the white men whose name was William. He was tall and lean with a shock of blond hair and he looked barely sixteen years old. He had a beautiful, symmetrical face and blue-grey eyes that could hold the gaze of anyone in the room. He carried himself with a studied composure that somehow set him apart, and something about him clicked with me. I had the impression that William fully recognised why and how he had landed up here and was striving to make the best of the situation whilst, at the same time, railing against it. I found myself wondering what it was like to be white in an overwhelmingly black prison, in a country with a recent history as violent and racist as South Africa's. I noticed myself relating to someone whose colour, just skin deep, was the same as mine.

I'd expected to see a visible difference between these people and me, to recognise something bad in them that I didn't share. But of course that wasn't true. Instead I met men who might have been my brother or son. They were shockingly articulate. Boys who had typically had very little love in their lives, who, with a depressing predictability, had lost their way, made terrible choices and done horrific things to other human beings. These were the lucky few who'd been selected by Khulisa as having sufficient education to pass the basic reading and writing requirements for a place on a rehab programme. They were here to discover, for the first time in their lives, who they were. They were boys who had never known a father, kids with an older brother dead from a gunshot and a mother who simply couldn't cope with what she'd given birth to. I had the impression of young men struggling to hold up a mirror, look themselves in the eye and find something to like in what they saw.

Several of the group began to trace their stories with me on that warm, close day in Sun City, shadow paths, dark and unkempt, deeply human both in their failings and in their small triumphs. I sat there with a lump in my throat and I thought about who I was and the beliefs I carried with me. I thought about the instinct to cut out what is rotten in society and toss it aside. I didn't want to simply run with the pack, to condemn someone and slam the door because they were somehow bad or outcast. To do so would have been to slam the door on a part of me as well. I had gone to South Africa to look for inspiration, both for my work and for myself. I found it here, in prison, in a form I hadn't expected, and it felt like an impulse to action.

~

Meanwhile, half a world away in southwest China, there lived another extraordinary leader who was to have a profound impact on my thinking. I first met Yang Xin in a small apartment in the city of Chengdu when Fields, Jason and I were there to prepare a Quest. Several people had told us about Yang Xin's work and eventually we'd tracked him down on the internet.

Chengdu's local moniker translates as "city of abundance" and it sits in a fertile plain, fed by the Yangtze River. But at the time of this, my first visit, the city was undergoing a startling transformation. The national government was hard at work promoting its "Go West" strategy to develop the western provinces of China, and Chengdu sat squarely in the middle of their plans. As a result, hundreds of thousands of farmers were in the midst of trading in a tough and muddy life on the land, and moving to homes in hastily erected tower blocks and jobs in factories, and on yet more construction sites, as the city swelled. It was as if several centuries had accidentally collided. Brash new buildings, of dubious architectural merit, sat beside ancient tea houses and temple gardens that were fragile pools of calm. Whole districts were being torn down to make way for new roads, apartments, cultural centres and software parks. Bicycles swarmed through the streets at rush hour like great armies of ants, despite a huge escalation of motor traffic. Shiny glass shop fronts, advertising global brands, jostled for space with dumpling stalls and impromptu posters promoting ear cleaning or blind man foot massage.

I felt somehow bereft and shaken by it all, though I couldn't say how. This was an example of China on the move, and little of it went unnoticed. In a land renowned for spicy food and a wealth of culture, Sichuan's musicians, poets and artists were at work, each depicting their own response to the tumultuous transitions underway with the precision of a scalpel peeling back skin. Fields, Jason and I had spent the morning in a disused factory, now home to a cluster of promising, emerging artists. They included men like Guo Wei, who was painting precocious teenagers in stark black and white, their heads a little too large, bodies a little too thin, their gaze, direct and defiant to mask a vulnerability; and Zhou Chunya who painted nothing but giant dogs on canvases as tall as the roof – ferocious dogs in green and red that lunged from the walls with raw power, eyes bulging, mouths wide and salivating.

We found the apartment which Yang Xin used as a base, tucked away in a nondescript part of the city, up several flights of concrete stairs. My expectations, as we climbed, were low and the day felt suddenly hard and grubby. A sign in Chinese read "Greenriver Environmental Protection Association", and so we knocked. The door was opened by a handsome man of medium build with long dark hair and a heavy near-black beard.

"Hello," he said in Chinese. "I'm Yang Xin."

He was wearing jeans and shirt and open-toed shoes and he ushered us into a small, sparsely furnished room with a desk and several battered chairs. We sat and began to introduce ourselves, explaining who we were, what we did and why we'd come. Yang Xin listened to us carefully, and then, with quiet understatement, he began to tell us about his work as founder of one of China's first environmental NGOs.

He'd established Greenriver, he said, in an effort to protect one of the most precious ecosystems on the planet, the high altitude, near pristine wilderness on the Qinghai-Tibetan plateau which stretched for thousands of miles across remote mountains and desert landscape. He and a small team of volunteers had established the Suonandajie Natural Ecological Protection Station. They'd named it after a colleague, killed in a one-man battle with some of the poachers who were pushing the Tibetan antelope to the brink of extinction.

"It was minus forty degrees when he died," Yang Xin said. "And by the time Suonan's body was found, it had frozen like an ice sculpture. He was holding a gun and surrounded by more than a thousand antelope skins he'd taken from the poachers."

Greenriver worked in partnership with indigenous nomadic people to protect their way of life and combat the impact of pollution and soil degradation. They were also beginning to study the Yangtze source area, in a bid to understand what was happening to the glaciers, and to learn how the rivers were faring downstream under the relentless push of industrialisation and population growth. The emerging picture was a grim one. But his work, he told us, in an unassuming, upbeat way, was about raising collective consciousness of the source area of some of the world's most important rivers.

"The mountains and glaciers of Qinghai and Tibet are the birth place of many rivers. They include the Yangtze and the Yellow River which flow across China, the Salween that flows on to Burma and Thailand, and the Mekong which is the water source for Yunnan province, Burma, Thailand, Laos, Cambodia and Vietnam. The Brahmaputra River also rises here, flowing through Assam and Bangladesh to join the Ganges in India. Together, these rivers support the lives of close to two billion people across south Asia."

In 1986, Yang Xin had organised an expedition by raft from the Yangtze's glacier source at some six thousand five hundred metres above sea level, to its mouth, almost four thousand kilometres away at the East China Sea – the longest river in Asia. It took one hundred and seventy days, and ten of his fellow explorers died on the journey. But it marked the beginning of a lifetime's work.

As they travelled through the towns and villages that line the river banks, Yang Xin stopped to ask the people who lived there whether they knew where the river came from, and where it was heading. Those he met at the start of the journey, who lived beside the tributaries, didn't know it as a single, vast river that crossed a continent. For them it was part of their own small ecosystem, a simple fact of life. The water flowed, heading who knew where. And many miles downstream, the people of Hubei knew only the big, broad swell of its curve as the river ran past, yielding what they needed and carrying away what they did not.

"I came to realise that no one knew the whole river. No one could see the whole picture. And I knew then what I was here to do," he said. "I would become an educator. My job was to teach people why the river mattered and how to take care of it. "

As I sat and listened to him, I looked about me at his stark, anonymous office. A hard-backed book caught my eye, tucked away on a high shelf. He finished speaking, and I pulled it down and began to turn the pages. It was Yang Xin's photographic account of the headwaters of the Yangtze River – page after page of breathtaking photographs, in an otherwise colourless room.

Here was the world's rooftop in vivid splendour: a wonderland of glaciers giving on to broad, layered landscapes where vast puddled ice melted across the plain. There were pictures of luminous lakes that mirrored the sky, cypress trees, windswept and proud, far above their natural altitude, and lichen, burnt orange and red rust, clinging to high, ragged rocks which towered over the flowered marshlands of the tundra. Yang Xin had captured the people of the plateau too, their burnished faces, tough and resilient, bodies wrapped in colour. These were the nomadic herdsmen of a glacial, awesome land, people who lived closer to the gods than most. Just another of the species for whom this place was home.

I looked from the photographs to Yang Xin and back again. We didn't speak the same language, but I knew what he was saying. He was expressing what I knew deep down and I felt profoundly grateful for it. His was a tale of connection with everything around him. I thought about his resolve to bridge a gulf and the pragmatic way he was going about it. I sat there weighing the painful incongruity of finding him here in another ugly tower block, in a city ripe with change and dense with fog and fumes, when his soul belonged outside.

I thought about the first time I had consciously begun to appreciate this kind of interconnectedness in nature. It had come to me whilst lying on my stomach in the woods in southwest England, staring at moss. I was there on a three-day course with the ecologist Stephan Harding, to learn about the environment. He'd asked us all to lie with our face six inches from the ground, and simply look at what was in front of our faces. I found myself looking at a carpet of moss – exquisite, tiny flowers of pinprick saffron encased in feathery ferns, puffs of spore capsules held aloft on spidery stems, and minute and perfect trumpets, bruised purple by the sun. They grew in dense, soft, rippling clumps in every shade of green and yellow.

In another setting I might have been marvelling at a different form of life, the microscopic intricacy of the human ear or the inner workings of the brain. The familiarity and similarity were uncanny. I was struck then, by the resemblance to a set of photographs I'd seen, taken from the Hubble telescope billions of light years from earth. As I'd looked at those images of space, I'd been overwhelmed with the sense that I was looking at a living thing – spirals of energy, miniscule yet huge, unfathomable and infused with light and colour.

Lying on the forest floor, I saw, in some sense for the first time, the wholeness that is life. It was a glimpse of beauty and mystery beyond anything my intellect could grasp, and I knew myself to be a part of it with a clarity and joy that went beyond anything I could give words to. I had the same feeling now, sitting in Yang Xin's bare, bleak office in Chengdu. He'd captured with his camera the inter-dependence of life. His photographs spoke of a man who knew who he was and where he belonged. Not in an inflated sense – it had nothing to do with ego. He was just another ordinary person doing extraordinary things. What he had to give, he shared through the poetry of pictures, with the humility of a man who had his feet sunk deep into the soil.

His story would stay with me. Over the years to come I returned regularly to see what Yang Xin was doing and to reflect on the lessons he, and others like him, had to share.

Chapter Three
Hidden Treasure

I n the centre of the south of India sits the garden city of Bangalore, now called Bengalaru. Celebrated for its temperate climate and the flowering trees that blossom in fiery orange, pinks and yellow each spring and summer, Bangalore is one of India's most demographically diverse and affluent cities, and the birthplace of many of its leading technology companies.

I first visited in 2001, as Sue and I prepared our initial India Quest. The city was, by then, truly hitting its stride, with five star hotels and sparkling office blocks rising from the dust. We spent our first few days immersed with some of the business process outsourcing (BPO) companies and software houses founded at the beginning of the nineties. The government of the time had responded to economic crisis by changing the foreign investment rules and triggering an inflow of overseas funds. As a new industry, software escaped much of the endless bureaucracy that had corrupted and stunted other business sectors for many years. As a result, an extraordinary transformation was now underway. This was India shining: world class entrepreneurs building global companies, multinationals setting up shop, immaculately-kept technology parks swarming with thousands of engineering graduates from the best universities in the country. Except for the back-up generators required to cope with frequent municipal power cuts, and the parking lots filled with two wheelers, these corporate campuses might easily have passed for Californian.

Several days into our visit, and seriously impressed by the talent and capabilities of those we had met so far, we turned our attention to the social sector in a city that looked a lot more prosperous than any other I'd seen in India. We wanted to explore what was going on further down the economic ladder, both amongst local people, many of whom remained relatively untouched by this newfound wealth, and amongst the hundreds of thousands of economic migrants who had flocked here from poor rural states to search for work. We asked around as to whom we should meet and one name that repeatedly came up was that of DM Naidu. With the help of a couple of email introductions, Sue and I tracked him down and arranged to go and see him at his office on the outskirts of the city.

"Come this afternoon!" he told us over the phone. "Call me when you're leaving your hotel and I'll explain to the taxi driver how to find us."

Our driver was local, but I'd long since learned that getting lost in one's own city was apparently a hazard of the job. We were soon subsumed in a tangle of unnamed lanes, stopping repeatedly for lengthy, animated conversations with street vendors and pedestrians. I phoned three times for fresh directions and Naidu repeated himself loudly down the phone both to me and the driver, in English and the local language, Kannada. Finally, we pulled up in front of a single-storey building and the taxi driver announced authoritatively that we'd arrived.

As we climbed out of the car, Naidu was there, waiting to greet us. "Welcome, welcome," he said slowly, smiling broadly. "We're so pleased you've come!"

Naidu was a man in late middle age, quite short, very dark skinned, with thick white hair and dressed in a white kurta. As he stepped forward to shake our hands I noticed his limp. One leg was significantly shorter than the other and he shuffled as he walked.

We left our shoes at the door and were ushered into an office that was clean and simply furnished, with two large windows left wide open to let the light pour in. I could sense something promising right away.

It wasn't only Naidu, it was his colleagues too. There was a softness and attentiveness about them and they received us with such warmth, it was as if we were the two people in the whole world they most wanted to see. Yet instinctively I knew that everyone who came here would be treated in just the same way. In the middle of the room stood a table spread with a cloth and set with a jug of water, cups and several small vases of flowers. The day was hot and a fan rattled and spun on the ceiling. Everything felt fresh and slow, as if time had paused. I recognised something gentle in Naidu. He brought a calming aura to the place.

We sat down with him and three of his co-workers, and began the introductions. They all belonged to an NGO called BasicNeeds, which worked to support and empower mentally ill people and their families. These were some of the most marginalised people in Indian society. Often they were ostracised by neighbours who found them disconcerting or frightening and wanted them gone or locked away. Many fell into destitution, taking their families down with them as they lost the capacity to earn a living. As Naidu spoke, I was struck by the deep respect he and his team shared for the people they served. He described, in careful detail, the effort they made to demystify mental health and involve every person in each step of their own journey as thoroughly as possible. It was a spontaneous response, nothing forced. In the absence of sufficient experienced medical staff, BasicNeeds was identifying and training local people to become informal health workers. The result was a robust and systematic approach that had spread from village to village across large swathes of India.

This first meeting with Naidu was to spark a bond which would become one of the most important influences in my life. Without really knowing it, I was in search of a wise friend, and I came to see him as a mentor. But he always refused the label. "I am not a teacher!" he used to say emphatically. "I too am learning from you!"

In time, I learned more about Naidu's life. He had never married and he lived with his brother, his brother's wife and their son Prajju, of whom Naidu was very proud. He'd been born, one of six children, in the small town of Ramireddypalli, in the state of Andhra Pradesh. Stricken with polio shortly after his first birthday, Naidu had become a "wounded healer".

"My greatest struggle as a child was to overcome the emotion I felt about my disability," he told me later. "But it gave me the gift to face all the other challenges that would come my way in life."

He had grown up an angry youth, fired by what he saw as injustice all around him. For a while he embraced Naxilism (militant Maoism practised in large areas of central India) until his best friend was killed in an encounter with the police.

"I decided then to renounce violence forever. I sought out spiritual teachers and in time I found my calling, which was to work with people with physical and mental disability," he said.

As I got to know Naidu in the years that followed, I would take the opportunity whenever I could, at the end of a Quest, to go and have a meal with him. We would talk about ideas and, as was his habit, he would often prepare some thought or other that he wanted to share with me, making notes about it before I arrived. There was a pattern to our conversations, things he asked me to pay attention to, little lessons he wished to impart, yet he always delivered them with meticulous humility and often a touch of irony.

"You're always coming and going Lindsay," he said to me on one such occasion, three years on from our first encounter in his office in Bangalore. "You get here, and things happen, but then you're gone again. I think you need to leave something behind."

It was a fair challenge. What could we leave behind that would be meaningful? Central to a Quest was the idea that a group of leaders travelled, usually from different continents, to meet with people in a given country and learn about life. To do this successfully, we needed to build relationships with all kinds of individuals, in the places we visited. Many of our hosts were influential business leaders, academics or the heads of civil society organisations, people who were interested in what we did and happy to exchange ideas. It wasn't too difficult to meet them in a way that made some sort of useful contribution. They enjoyed the interaction with whomever we brought with us because in many ways they were peers, fellow leaders and part of the establishment, informal or otherwise. They could explain who they were and what they did, ask questions, share expertise and make new, often long-lasting, connections with one another.

But Quests also included time with some of the poorest communities, with whom it sometimes felt like another story. This was not because the relationships between visitors and hosts were awkward (they rarely were), but simply because the economic gap was so wide.

These were people who typically looked forward to meeting us, often very much so. There was value and pride in talking about their lives and what they were doing to change them, with a group of leaders who had typically travelled a long way to be there. We frequently left with a request to return as soon as possible, a sense of spirits lifted and a renewed belief in one another. Over and over, we found an abundance of some of the most important qualities in life: generosity, perseverance, compassion. Time and time again, we encountered resourcefulness and creativity. In many ways these people were rich. Yet they were usually economically very poor, with little or no access to the means to transform their own lives and those of their children. Too often, we met families locked into a cross-generational cycle of poverty and, when the Quest ended, we walked away and returned to our respective homes.

"What can you leave behind, Lindsay?" Naidu asked. "Why only work with powerful leaders, who already have so many resources?"

~

In the city of Mumbai, meanwhile, some six hundred miles northwest of Bangalore, our mutual friend Sujata Khandekar was asking similar questions. A passionate and effective advocate for the poor, Sujata saw potential in people where others did not. She'd spent the best part of twenty years working as an activist, building a grassroots-led organisation named CORO, with the goal of improving the quality of life of hundreds of thousands of marginalised women and children in Mumbai. What started out as a project to raise female literacy, developed steadily into a much broader effort to empower people with the skills and confidence to stand up for themselves and change their own circumstances.

Unlike Naidu, Sujata had been born a Brahmin, a member of the highest Hindu caste. But she insisted that CORO must evolve to be entirely led by Dalits (formerly known as "untouchables" – people at the bottom of the caste system) and others from disadvantaged backgrounds. She had a tough determination about her, a quiet stubbornness, and she defined success as working herself out of a job.

Naidu and Sujata joined forces to challenge us. They wanted us to come up with a shared vision for a leadership initiative for the poorest in society. They'd observed the difference a Quest could make to participants, most of whom were influential people. Now they wanted to help us do the same for undiscovered leaders.

We decided to create a parallel programme to Quests, slightly different in nature and adapted to the circumstances of those for whom it was designed. The concept was a twelve-month "fellowship" for promising emerging leaders in some of the countries we visited on Quests. It would be a leadership development programme tailored to their needs, part-time (twenty five hours per week) and delivered locally. It had to be cost effective and modular, so that fellows could continue to earn a living and look after their families during the process – a kind of "university in the community". Each fellowship comprised training, extensive mentorship and support. The programme included project planning, research and analysis, communication skills and advocacy. Every fellow was asked to pick a subject on which to focus, such as sanitation, livelihoods, education or domestic violence. They were required to undertake a nine-month project working with no fewer than five hundred families in their own locality. It called for long hours, resilience and dedication.

The vision was to seek out those with the capacity to tackle tough issues. The need was obvious and the programme had to be flexible and creative in order to reach some of the most disadvantaged in society. We wanted to focus on "invisible" leaders, regardless of status or gender. This meant accessing people with poor or non-existent literacy skills, who typically remained unseen in the economic system. In a way, we were challenging conventional models of education. Here were people without very much of it, who knew what was good for them and what they wanted for the future. They knew it as well as anyone from the most elite schools and universities in the world.

Guided by Sujata and Naidu, a pilot fellowship programme was launched in 2004, supported by other local mentors with whom we'd built trust and a shared sense of purpose. Chris Underhill, a serial social entrepreneur and Naidu's co-founder at Basicneeds, joined us as the Chair of the newly-created Leaders' Quest Foundation, the charitable body we formed to fund the work. Without realising it, we had taken the next step in building a global community that would truly reflect humanity in all its extremes. It included many people with status and influence. But just as important were those whose lives lay closer to the edge, be they homeless street vendors or women struggling to put a single meal in front of their families every day.

There is something powerful in demonstrating that leaders can emerge from all kinds of circumstances and stand toe-to-toe with anyone else. It's an idea that most people agree with in theory, yet it rarely truly comes to pass. Fellowships are about opportunity and, like Quests, they are also about asking provocative questions about priorities and the way influence and power are shared.

~

In the meantime, all of this had to be paid for, somehow. Our business model had always been self-funding. We invested time in researching content, themes and ideas and then going out and meeting with people, all well in advance of each Quest. We talked with people about what we had to offer and encouraged them to get involved, whether as participants or as hosts. Often, we invited someone to join a Quest regardless of their ability to pay. Those who could afford the full price did so, whilst others from NGOs, social enterprises and the like, came on bursaries or scholarships. We were mission- rather than profit-driven and the diversity of people on a Quest was important. What we really cared about was impact.

It was a balancing act to ensure we generated the necessary income to cover all of our costs and invest in the future. Money was a constant worry, but it was probably a healthy one. Financial pressure kept our feet firmly on the ground. It required that we pay attention to doing what we were most passionate about, whilst ensuring we could pay the bills and sustain ourselves. When the two coincided (they frequently did), and we found ourselves paid for doing what we thought was valuable, it was a welcome boost.

The fellowship, however, called for a different model, given that it was directed at people who were almost always financially poor. To bring the programme to life, we would have to raise funds. At first it wasn't difficult because we started out on a modest scale. But as we moved forward with a plan to train six hundred fellows in India and China over the next three years, it became clear we would have to refocus on fundraising.

One of the first people to whom I reached out for help was an American entrepreneur named David Weekley. On the surface he was far from an obvious choice, for my first meeting with him a couple of years earlier in London had been something of a disaster.

I'd been invited as a guest speaker to meet a group of business leaders who were all part of a rather exclusive international club, in town to attend a meeting at the Savoy Hotel. I arrived mid-morning as instructed, negotiated my way past the reception staff and went in search of the room where I was due to speak. I wandered along various corridors until I came upon a sign with my name on it outside a large meeting room. Inside, rows of empty seats were laid out and a buffet table stood laden with pastries and canapés. The carpet was thick-pile velvet, dense and busy blue, and the ceiling hung with heavy chandeliers. A handful of people were picking at food from the table and talking amongst one another. I stood for a while, until someone showed up who was apparently expecting me.

"You just start when you're ready," he said. "People will come and go, listening to the sessions they're most interested in."

I waited for the room to fill, but it didn't, and eventually a scattering of people sat down. There were, it seemed, several competing sessions with riveting speakers in the rooms next door. My own seemed remarkably poorly attended and I had the impression that no one wanted to hold my eye. I stood up, introduced myself and started to speak – to describe what we did and why. One member of the audience got up rather noisily and left the room. Others went back for a second round of canapés. I pressed on. A couple of generous questions came my way and then simply petered out. I began to cross the stage to leave. I was demoralised, but also strangely amused by the whole episode. It was my own fault. I had misread the audience, failed to connect with them and failed to be the bridge I hoped to be. Yet there was a dynamic in the room that made it doubly hard and I felt, as I often did, as though I was in an upside down world. Upside down because, collectively, it seemed as if we'd somehow got our values wrong. Making money was apparently the primary focus of the people here and they had proved themselves remarkably good at it. Yet I had the impression that many of them had lost touch with the ordinary world around them. Even speakers invited to this annual event were simply a service, another form of entertainment. Mid-way across the stage, I decided to say what I felt. I turned and walked back to the microphone.

"Do you mind if I give you some feedback?" I asked.

Now I had their attention. Everyone looked at me. Someone coughed with their mouth full and nodded yes.

"This hasn't felt like a great process," I said. "I pitch up to meet you and to speak and it feels very unwelcoming. It's not as if I'm paid to be here, so it seems a shame for it to feel so bad. There's no one to say hello or even explain the proceedings. You all seem to be wandering about eating. If we treated the people we meet on Quests this way, we wouldn't exist. We'd never get invited back. I hope this may be helpful to you when you design your next conference. Thank you very much and have a great day."

I left the stage and was heading for the door when a man in an open-necked shirt and chinos stood up and cleared his throat heavily, an amused and awkward smile on his face.

"Lindsay!" he said. "My name is David Weekley and it is my distinct pleasure, on behalf of all of us, to thank you most sincerely for joining us here today. I would like to present you with this gift as a token of our appreciation." It came out in a deep southern drawl – American, but I wasn't sure where from (it was Texas, I learned later).

I climbed back onto the stage. I wasn't embarrassed. It just felt rather funny. "Thank you," I said.

"You know I'd like to come on one of your Quests one day," he replied.

"Sure...that would be great," I said, and left the stage carrying a rather bulky gift wrapped flamboyantly in red and gold paper. I headed for the ladies toilet where I found an attendant, dressed in a black uniform and white apron.

"Would you like this?" I asked her, proffering the gift.

She looked at me startled, as if I had invited her to dance or take her clothes off.

"Here, please, take it! You have it," I said, and foisted it into her hands. I left the ladies room, crossed the hotel lobby, walked out into the street and wandered around for a while before heading for the Tube.

Later, I called Fields. "That was a horrible experience," I told her. "I hated it! I never want to do it again. Remind me never to do it again. It just felt so ... arrogant."

A few months on, David called out of the blue. "Can I come to China?" he asked.

He did, and then he came to India a year or so later. His home town, it turned out, was Houston and he was a self-made businessman who'd been highly successful in house-building. He was the only American on that China Quest and, at the end of the day in the hotel bar, he responded with grace and humour to the full force of our European contingent, who were delighted to get their teeth stuck into someone from the US (better still, a real Republican from Texas!), whom they could hold to account for the world's collective woes.

I liked David very much and we subsequently became friends. I was intrigued at how he ran his business and his life. There was a kind of uncompromising urgency and dedication about him. I wondered where it came from and I asked him.

"I've been given many extraordinary opportunities," he told me. "I'm very blessed. I've had an easy life in many ways ... I didn't create these gifts, they came to me. I simply want to do the best with what I have, to use it all as wisely as I can."

David was, I learned, a generous and committed philanthropist. And he was also tough. In 2008 as we geared up to grow the fellowship programme I asked for his support. His eye for detail was intense and he bombarded me with ideas and questions, sent at all hours of the day and night: "How much does it cost per fellow? How many lives do each one influence? What are the outcomes? Can you prove it?"

He was totally focused on measuring impact (he was right to ask) and I struggled with this, partly no doubt because we weren't yet good enough at capturing it, and partly because I thought it risked missing the point. I worried that we would reduce our work to a pile of statistics and miss out on everything that wasn't easily counted. We argued back and forth and finally I thought I'd lost the fight. We had a phone call and he told me he didn't think he could fund us. Although I probably had no right to do so, I simply told him how I felt. The words more or less tumbled out.

"I'm just very, very disappointed," I said.

A little while later, David called me back. "I believe in what you're doing, I've thought about it and I've decided I'd like to back you. You can always expect me to ask tough questions but I'd like to support you."

It was a generous gift at a vital time and we launched the next chapter of the fellowships, just as we had hoped to do.

~

About nine months after the programme started, I went back to Bangalore and arranged with Naidu to meet a group of the fellows to see how they were progressing. The meeting would take the form of a workshop with a visiting Quest group of business and civil society leaders.

We fixed a date and Naidu hired a meeting room at a local hotel and arranged for some of the fellows to travel (some of them for a day or more) to join us. While I had read their profiles and knew a fair amount about the work they did, I hadn't yet met any of them. These were people who had been hand-picked by Naidu and the panel of interviewers he had recruited – all part of the exacting process to win a place on the programme, in the face of heavy demand. I was excited to have the chance to meet them and see what they were doing. I arrived together with the visitors at the appointed hour, to find nine fellows waiting for us, along with Naidu and another mentor named Nandini, who worked for one of our partner organisations, ActionAid.

As we walked into the room, Naidu stepped forward with his customary up-down limp, a big smile and an enthusiastic exclamation of "Great, Lindsay, great!" by way of greeting.

The introductions began, in a mixture of Hindi, Kannada, Konkani, Marathi and English. A handful of people spoke all the languages, most spoke two or three, and we visitors, only one. Multiple translations were required in a kind of synchronised swim that was perfectly pitched, deeply respectful and patient, and interspersed with waves of laughter as each person caught up with the proceedings. Three of the assembled group were blind, including Nandini. Three were disabled, two severely. One gentleman had a leg that stuck out at right angles to his body. He walked on crutches, clearing a path before him as he went. Another, named Venky, sat scrunched in a small ball on a straight-backed chair, all four limbs curled up and close to useless. He was also blind.

As the meeting progressed I watched those with sight keep physical contact with those without, painting for them in words the details they couldn't see, and guiding their hands to the food when lunch was served. Those of us without language were constantly included in the discussion, each nuance carefully translated. We learned that Venky had mobilised some two thousand people across his rural community to tackle the stigma of mental illness and help families who had sunk, sometimes to the point of destitution, as their key breadwinner was overcome by depression or schizophrenia. It had required two days travel for him to come to meet us. How he did any of this was beyond our comprehension until we heard him speak. He made us understand that anything was possible. The air seemed to fizz with a warm, life-giving glow that simply swept any obstacles out of the way.

I sat through the encounter, swaying somewhere between tears and a big, stupefied smile. The Quest group looked suitably taken aback, but rallied graciously to hide their surprise and enter into the joy and inspiration of it all. The day felt light and beautiful and I wanted to laugh at the delicious irony of it all. I was elated to be there and to look on, as several of my own assumptions were unceremoniously tipped upside down and scattered like marbles across the floor. The idea, for instance, buried somewhere in my sub-conscious, that you had to be able-bodied to lead, or that you needed sight to inspire. I'd had no idea that any of our fellows were blind, disabled or both. These kinds of issues were not part of the selection process so there was no reason to know, and the likelihood had never entered my head.

And of course Naidu knew this. This was him at work, both his sharp, earthy wit and his big spirit, forever testing boundaries. A simple teacher, no words required. Just another lesson, exquisitely delivered.

Chapter Four
Return of the Soul

"India's like an injured person lying on the floor," said Lin Lin. "All the wounds are visible and open to the air, and blood is flowing into the ground. But here in China, all our wounds are on the inside."

We were sitting together in a cafe in Beijing's art district. Lin Lin, usually so stoic and contained, was crying, her face pale. We'd finished a Quest the previous day and were both slowly unpacking our thoughts about the week.

Lin Lin had grown up in the city of Dalian in northeast China. In the course of her three years with Leaders' Quest, she'd become accustomed to sharing her country with visitors who often arrived fearful and suspicious of this vast and growing nation. Some came eager to pierce the veil and see, others to reaffirm their own preconceptions. Six weeks previously, Lin Lin had made her first visit to India where, like many Chinese people, she'd been shocked at the chaos and blatant poverty in many of the streets and the apparent incapacity of government to do anything more than get in the way. Now, back home, the contrasts were more complicated, the answers less clear.

Of all the countries where we work, China is the one where I find it hardest to hold an open mind. The omnipresent authority of government and the speed and irreversibility of change frighten me. When I first went to visit the municipality of Chongqing in the southwest, three days into my trip, I could still scarcely comprehend what I was seeing. The scale of building took my breath away. There were literally thousands of tower blocks under construction. I couldn't compute it – the notion of so many people on the move, families and cultures dislocated, and the colossal impact on the earth.

On my final afternoon in the city I went to visit a group of "green volunteers" – environmental champions who were pioneering education programmes for schools and businesses. The taxi driver got lost on the way, complaining that the streets were changing by the week, and we arrived an hour late. I took the elevator part way up a rather bleak tower block until it broke down, then climbed several flights of concrete stairs and knocked on a door with a small green sign outside. It was opened by a middle-aged man in spectacles who greeted me with a warm handshake, brushed aside my apology for being so late, and ushered me inside. The apartment was cramped but light and evidently served as both office and home. Stacks of newspapers, boxes of spent batteries, crates of plastic bottles and a huge pile of old clothes took up half the room.

"Recycling!" he said with a cheerful laugh as we made our way to seats by the window. He introduced me to three of his colleagues, a woman and two men, all of whom seemed enthusiastic to meet and start a dialogue.

I sat down and began to listen to this group of activists as each one told their story, but I couldn't really concentrate. My eyes kept wandering to the window, some sixteen storeys up, which looked out over their particular quarter of Chongqing. I felt my face freeze in a kind of daze that I couldn't hide. It was as if we were sitting on a tiny raft made of plastic bottles, looking at an oncoming tsunami. The man in spectacles followed my gaze, out over the vast and foggy tangle of chaotic tower block construction as far as the eye could see. And then he looked at me with half a smile.

"Ah yes," he said, nodding slowly and waving his arms wide. "We are at home even here. We have our own forest just outside the window!"

I looked out over that undulating urban ocean and I tried to see it through his eyes. What must it feel like to be a passionate environmentalist in the midst of so much turmoil? And what did the same view look like through the eyes of the migrant workers who were constructing all the buildings, the government planners presumably figuring it all out, or the farmers, moving to an apartment in the city? Some, I knew, came willingly, others not, all part of a huge, coordinated effort to urbanise and transform the nation. My own ground felt far less certain in that moment than when I'd arrived. I felt as if I was looking at a giant tangled ball of string. So many different points of view were possible and I simply wanted to acknowledge in myself that it was OK not to have an answer. Should this kind of development stop, slow down, proceed in a different way? Instinct told me it was completely unsustainable. But who was I to say? What kind of deep reflection and dialogue was needed to plot a way forward in a country of this magnitude? What hidden parts of ourselves did we need to engage when confronting these kinds of dilemmas? To cut through the competing claims as to what was right and wrong, supported by often contradictory facts, and to let some intuition in? Where was the place for the soul in all of this, as well as the intellect?

I spent the evening alone, mulling over the day. I felt as if I was in an in-between place. Life here seemed so unrelenting, like the scrape of metal on bone. I felt fear and a kind of sad unease. It was not fear of people or politics. Rather it had to do with Nature, as if rivers could be made to run backwards by sheer force of will and the power of numbers, and the earth itself could be turned inside out by mankind. At the same time, I felt appreciation for the people I'd met and the struggle of so many millions to build a decent life. I wanted to understand, to connect despite the differences, and to engage here with the same passion and energy as I had back home.

~

Over the course of many trips to China in the years that followed that first visit to Chongqing, one of the people who most inspired me was Jin Xing. Jin had been born in 1967 in Laoying province in the north, to a Korean father and a Chinese mother. His father was a policeman and as a child Jin attended a local elementary school and began to attract attention as a bright student and a promising gymnast and dancer. At the age of nine, Jin was recruited into the Peoples' Liberation Army, moved away from home, and began an intensive programme of dance and military training, eventually attaining the rank of Colonel as a leading member of the military dance troupe. But under the surface, Jin was wrestling with a profound dilemma. Born into a boy's body, from his earliest years, he had felt himself to be a girl.

Jin hid his feelings and his career took off, first in China and then overseas. And then, in 1996, after several successful years in Europe and the US training and working with some of the world's leading choreographers, Jin Xing returned home to undergo sex reassignment surgery and become the country's first officially recognised transsexual. The decision to have the operation in China was a conscious one. Jin wanted to come home to make a choice, supported by family and friends, and openly challenge her homeland to recognise her for who she was. A few months later, as she took to the stage once again, the person who had been widely hailed as the country's leading contemporary male dancer, emerged as its leading female one.

Jin Xing went on to marry, adopt three children and launch her own independent dance company. She was uncompromisingly individual with a deft capacity to shock. Her goal was to bring dance to a new generation, and to use her craft to give expression to what she saw unfolding across the country.

Several years after we first met, as I was planning another Quest to China, she invited a group of us to come and join her company in rehearsal. We were to see a new piece they were preparing. I knew nothing about the performance, but I knew it would be special and we agreed a date to meet in the main studio of the Shanghai Theatre.

The day began, however, in a different way. We'd scheduled to visit a factory and meet with the management of one of the largest manufacturers of white label electronics goods for some of the biggest global brands. The business designed and made personal computers, laptops and mobile phones, products that had literally changed the world over the preceding twenty years, connecting and empowering millions of people in the process. Materials and components from around the globe had been mined, made and shipped here to be assembled into devices which had become vital tools of everyday life. The factory was another link in an intricate supply chain, driven by the constant churn of innovation, relentless demand to slice cost and turn out the next best thing – smaller, sleeker, faster. We were there to see for ourselves what people meant when they referred to China as "the workshop for the world", to spend some time in discussion with the company's leaders about their strategy, in what was a hugely competitive market, and to begin to understand the economic and social impact of manufacturing on the country.

After breakfast, eight of us set out for the manufacturing complex on the outskirts of the city. The scale of the enterprise was astonishing. Uniform, symmetrical, grey buildings were immaculately laid out in a huge and sprawling grid system, neatly divided by spotlessly clean roads, all lined with long rows of identical orange and yellow flowers. The campus was home to tens of thousands of workers, the majority of whom lived on-site in dormitories. State-of-the-art facilities housed a whole ecosystem for employees, most of them young women, prized for their attention to detail. They'd been recruited in mind-boggling numbers from small towns and villages across the country.

We visited one of a number of hangar-like factory units. Inside, the production line stretched so far into the distance that the people manning it seemed to disappear into tiny, moving pixels. Everyone was dressed in identical white coats and triangular headscarves of sky blue. Some were seated on stools, while others stood, all eyes fixed on the procession of laptops moving rhythmically along the conveyor belt in front of them. Every worker had his or her own role to play. Twelve seconds of dextrous hand movements attaching tiny parts to a circuit board. And as each one passed, the next arrived. Another twelve seconds of rapid precision. Then another, and another. It looked like a great, soundless orchestra with everyone in perfect sync.

We watched, mesmerised, as the computers moved steadily along the line. Some had white stickers on them, with the name of an end customer, his or her exact requirements, and the final shipping address. Bruce Wilson of Cincinnati's laptop was being assembled before my eyes, and unbeknownst to its future owner, an invisible thread was quietly unfurling, linking him with so many young women who had crossed half a continent in search of a job. They were living a new life, very different to that of their parents and the generations before them, each of them contributing their own special twelve seconds of life to the birth of Mr Wilson's laptop.

Later, after lunch, we left the campus and travelled across the city to meet Jin Xing and her self-funded company of five. These child-women too had crossed a continent to fulfil a dream. They wanted to dance and had no means of support. They'd arrived, like many others, on Jin Xing's doorstep, each from a different place with a unique history, and asked her to teach them. The most promising she took under her wing, supported with basic accommodation and food, and taught with a rigour and passion that would prove a wonderful gift.

As we walked into the studio, Jin Xing stopped mid-sentence to look up, then waved us to come forward, pointing to some stools beside the open stage. We slipped off our shoes, crossed the dance floor to take our seats, and as we did so, I began to feel the beauty of the space wash over me. Light streamed through big panes of glass set in a cavernous, curved roof, then bounced off the walls, bathing the room in bright white. The setting was informal, drenched in concentration. Dancers stretched their bodies in preparation, each lost in their own inner world. A sound engineer sat on the floor, playing with an improbably small cassette player and speakers, searching for the right place in the music.

The piece they were preparing was called "Made in China – Return of the Soul". Five young women, from the provinces of Mongolia, Yunnan and Hebe, were about to engage in a dance that would speak of the juxtaposition between factory life and the unseen world of the heart. Head high, voice sharp and clear, Jin Xing told them what she expected in rapid, staccato Chinese. Then, she fell silent for a moment, before signalling with a slight bow of her head for the performance to begin.

We entered an imaginary factory of smooth steel, sharp-edged and precisely engineered. The dancers stepped forward and began to move, slowly at first, like winding clocks coming to life. Then faster and faster, their mechanical rhythm swift and clean, bodies merging with machines, until you couldn't tell where one began and the other ended. The awkward bend and turn of a screw and the tight, tight discipline of tap, tap, tap, repeat – a perfect copy every time. Here was a contemporary vision of a familiar story – industrialisation, the meeting of men, women and technology, born of our own ingenuity. It was a dance that portrayed the quest for a new form of security, beyond the vagaries of climate, the steady rise of material consumption and the upward climb of yet another generation. It was not a judgement, but a commentary on a complex world. Yet it did contain a question, asking us to pause and pay attention.

Time slowed again and the factory line froze. Seconds passed in stillness, save for the gentle rise and fall of breath. There was an explosion of energy as the dancers took flight across the stage. Spinning, whirling, they swooped like birds in perfect formation, casting shadows on the dappled floor, then seemed to fly towards the rafters and hover in the sunlight, dazzling. Strong limbs, brown and pale, brushed the sky, as if to touch the world, and in some small way to shape it too. This was a dance of freedom and love, the soul returning home. It spoke of a purity rooted somewhere ancient and the spirit drawn to a flame. Five young women were playing out the dreams that bind us, beyond the splintered difference of language, culture and caste. They'd left their families behind them to realise who they were. They were telling a story, at once familiar and new, about what it is to be alive and to deeply rejoice in living.

At the end we sat quite still, lost in what we'd witnessed. I could feel the breadth of the gap they had bridged and it touched a wound inside. I felt the divide between my head and my heart. China was not foreign after all, but a mirror. I sat there beside the stage, shocked at our collective brilliance and the price to be paid. And I thought about our drive to forge ahead and the squeezing out of some of our own essence in the rush.

~

Leaders' Quest progressed and so did our thinking about what we were really offering. A Quest often brought to life the realities of capitalism and globalisation in different parts of the world. Sometimes we witnessed the best of the human spirit at work. We discovered ingenious, life-changing innovations from companies engaged in fields as diverse as software development, house-building or healthcare. We saw new jobs created, young people brought into the workplace, and inspiring training programmes to help them get started. Often we met people who were realising their true aspirations for the first time in their lives. And sometimes we saw the other side of the same coin: the impact of untrammelled self-interest and greed, both individual and collective.

I grew familiar, for example, with conversations with factory owners about the health and safety shortcuts taken by many of their customers (including global retail brands) to reduce costs or speed up production. It seemed to be an easy pattern to fall into, facilitated by the use of intermediaries who took away the sense of personal accountability. If you hired independent auditors or middlemen to act on your behalf, it wasn't so difficult to turn a blind eye to money passed under the table or pressure applied to vulnerable people. I'd hoped I would find that the stories of poor management and malfeasance were exaggerated, but the truth is, I did not. It was not a case of east versus west, north versus south, one culture against another. Rather, it was a case of the worst of human nature versus the best of it, and the need for resilience and determination to embed good practice within businesses, governments and NGOs alike. We were learning how to help people think about the impact of bad behaviour and also show the cumulative positive outcomes that flowed when people did the right thing.

I thought about how personal all of this was. It wasn't about someone else out there, driven by a system over which ordinary people had no influence. The economy, working conditions, everyday experiences – all of these were shaped by the individual choices we made in our workplace, our buying habits, the way we treated our neighbours. How different might the world look if we thought of ourselves as fellow citizens rather than employees or consumers?

We realised that we wanted to be engaged with systemic as well as personal change. This would include working more closely with business as a way to bridge the gap between the choices made by individuals and the organisations they are part of. It was about exploring the soul of a company, thinking about its responsibility as an entity, and the role of the individuals within it, in setting direction and living out their values in their work lives as well as at home.

At this point, in the middle of 2004, I received a call from Steven Tallman, one of the senior partners at Bain and Company, the firm where I had begun my career.

"I've heard good things about what you're doing, Lindsay. It sounds really interesting," he said. "So, I have a question for you. Next year, we plan to take our global partner group to Shanghai for a meeting. I wonder if you can turn it into a short Quest, help us understand China and get a sense of life on the ground. The only thing is, we've grown quite a bit. There are two hundred and fifty partners now. Can you manage that?"

I paused, just for a moment. The largest programme we'd run so far was for around twenty five people, divided into smaller groups of eight or nine each day. This was rather different.

"No problem," I replied. "We'd love to do it."

The following spring, with a growing team of colleagues, we ran our first corporate programme, for Bain, with twenty five different streams of visits and meetings, a mass of complexity and very little sleep for many weeks beforehand. But it worked. We were off on the next wave of figuring out how we could be effective. Over the next few years, what we came to call "tailored Quests" grew to occupy some eighty percent of our schedule, as we found more and more businesses interested in engaging with the world in a different way.

We learned that working with companies, however, could be a mixed blessing. It was exhilarating to see what was possible and to dig deep with people, to find what they most cared about, and then work out how these things, too, could be reflected in what they did. And at the same time it was frustrating and disappointing to watch so many firms move at a glacial pace. Many struggled when it came to figuring out their purpose beyond making money, usually because their leaders had chosen to switch off their innate capacity to look beyond what could be quantified.

Sometimes the disappointment felt horrible. A year or two after the first Bain Quest, I was back in China, this time with one of the big private equity firms which were at the peak of their power before the financial meltdown, apparently masters of the universe. We'd just finished a closing session, reflecting on what everyone had learned and the impressions and insights they would take home. I knew we'd helped individuals to make progress, but we hadn't really moved the business as a whole. The group had asked for the week to finish in spectacular fashion and everyone was gathered for drinks on the terrace of a funky red-lit bar on Shanghai's most famous street, the Bund. I was standing, momentarily alone, looking out over a breathtaking view of high rise swagger, mesmerising lights, and the Huangpu River spread out beneath us like a ribbon in the dark, when I spotted the CEO wandering towards me. Without looking up from his BlackBerry he said with a sneer and an awkward toss of his head, "I don't think you've added much value to me or my firm."

He had, in fact, missed the entire Quest we'd designed for his company. Too preoccupied doing deals, he'd stayed locked away in his hotel room. I sensed my presence made him uneasy, like a bad dream loitering in the back of the brain. I'd been so busy on the Quest that I'd barely slept for three days and I felt crushed by his disdain.

Suddenly, I was seized by an absurd and murderous desire. I wanted to pick him up, throw him over my shoulder like some huge sack of flour, and hurl him from the balcony. I pictured him taking flight, out across the star-spangled Bund with its fairy lights and its six lanes of traffic and all the glittering people below. I could see them watching from the pavements, rooted to the spot and looking up in voyeuristic horror, as he flew in a perfect arc right over their heads, to land in the middle of the Huangpu, sending huge rainbow showers up into the night sky like firework rockets. It was just the kind of spectacular ending he'd asked for.

Instead, I took my white hot fury, squelched it tight into a ball of dark matter, and swallowed. I fumbled in my mind for a reply. His eyes stayed locked on the BlackBerry screen, fingers tapping hard upon the keys. Eventually, I said something undignified and inappropriate – I don't remember what – and turned on my heels. A few steps later I slunk into the shadows, in tears like a spoilt child, angry and bitterly disappointed not to have made more of a mark. But I was also sad for him. I felt as if I was looking at a man separated from some core part of who he was, cut off from the world, despite his power and wealth. I found it hard to witness the vehemence with which he held the waves at bay, testimony perhaps to the depth of his fear. It just felt like a great big wasted opportunity.

~

A few months after this encounter, I was back in China, this time in Beijing, with a group of business leaders from Europe, Africa and Asia. Once again, many of them were in private equity. They made their money buying companies, with the goal of increasing their value and then selling them on a few years later. They were with us, not only to learn more about China, but also to ask some robust questions about the role of their industry in the world, and the part they played in it.

Our pattern for the week was to split into small teams for a series of different visits and then to come together as a whole each evening, to talk about what we'd seen. The first day began at dawn with a Tai Chi master in the gardens of the Temple of Heaven. Much to the amusement of a widening circle of onlookers, we were there for a lesson and were struggling, ineptly, to keep up with our teacher as the city awoke. Afterwards we travelled to Tsinghua University, to meet with some of the faculty and then with a group of students. They were all smart, ambitious and full of challenging questions about how we'd got to where we were in life.

Lunch followed in a nearby family restaurant – an eclectic affair, set at a big round table in a bright room of red and gold, with a multitude of dishes coming and going. With us were a journalist, an internet entrepreneur, a drama teacher and an economist from the mining industry. Over noodles, the economist shared awe-inspiring statistics on Chinese demand for natural resources and the likely geopolitical, environmental and economic impact of it all.

We were to spend the afternoon with a local NGO whose purpose was to protect the rights of migrant workers. Tensions between urban and rural people – including migrants to city jobs who came from the countryside and often remained outsiders – were increasingly apparent in China at the time, and a source of widespread unease. There were already an estimated one hundred and sixty million rural labourers working in cities with temporary rights to remain, and this figure was predicted to more than double over the next decade. These were all people contributing, in one way or another, to the booming economy. Yet many of them lived precarious, stressful lives, with little hope for the future.

The NGO's office was a traditional house built around a courtyard. It was tucked away down a narrow, winding street in one of the few remaining old parts of the city. We had to walk the last several hundred yards to the door as the road was too narrow to drive along. As we reached the door, one of the Quest group turned to me and said, "So Lindsay, tell me, how do you measure the impact of what you do?"

It was a familiar question and a fair one. "I'm happy to answer," I said. "But let's talk about it after the visit."

The door opened and the greetings began. Waiting for us in the inner courtyard was the softly spoken, passionate founder of the organisation. A lawyer by training, he'd grown to be an influential, and sometimes challenging, advisor to both business and government on migrant labour issues. With him were a group of around twenty young men and women. Most of them worked on construction sites or in restaurant kitchens, with a few also employed in factories. They lived in an uncompromising environment, where legal rights for workers often had yet to be established and those that existed were frequently ignored. None of them spoke English and, with the exception of my colleague Lanying and two of our group, we didn't speak Chinese.

Outside, in the small courtyard garden, it was cold, but the sun shone. A couple of the migrants invited us to introduce ourselves. They wanted us to do so with hand signals and movements, no words allowed. The visitors were a bit taken aback, at risk of feeling silly or conspicuous, but someone took the lead and broke the ice. Another short game followed which none of us could quite master, but which involved running round in circles chasing one another. People began to laugh and the tension fell away.

The introductions over, we crowded into the small office for a performance that the migrants had prepared for us. Tables were pushed back against the wall to clear a space for the stage, and we settled together on low stools in a couple of tightly packed rows to wait for the play to begin. It was to be a mime. A girl stepped forward into the empty space. Deft and silent, she took us back in time. With graceful hand movements, she conjured up the home where she'd grown up with her parents and grandmother, two rooms of brick and clay, and the green and muddy fields in which it sat. The fireplace for a biting winter, and the double wok her mother used to cook– one for the family and one for the chickens and the pig.

The girl packed a few belongings and prepared to leave. She didn't want to go, and they didn't want to lose her, but she had to earn a living and the time had come. The whole village cried as she left, but she hid her own tears and bottled them up inside. Painfully, she began to drag herself across the stage, a thousand miles or more, to the other side.

And then, desolate, she curled up in a ball and lay still upon the floor.

Two men barged in from nowhere, rough and coarse. They pulled the girl to her feet, grabbed her hard and pinned her to the wall, their faces pushed up far too close to hers. Hands rifled through her clothes and pressed into her flesh. They hit her again and again, too troubling to count the blows, then thumped her hard and threw her to the ground. They'd bought her like a sack of coal and the truth of it weighed heavily in the room.

Others came forward to join the girl on the cold stone floor. A multiplying human huddle, everyone with their own tale of leaving held inside, faces cast with the certainty of loss. They left little trails of crumbs across the ground to remind them where they'd come from.

It was damp and dirty and the food was scarce. They were not alone, but everyone was lonely. Employers came and went, scanning their wares, picking out a strong, young man here and there, with the promise of a handful of yuan, sometimes snatching the money away when the job was done. One of the migrants worked in construction. All day long he shimmied up and down bamboo scaffolding, carrying bricks and labouring in the sky. Then one day he lost his balance. He fell and landed with a sickening thud upon the stone. His leg no longer moved and you knew at once it would not heal. A rigid, useless limb for life, he went unpaid even for the final fateful job.

Some of the workers were crying and they meant it. We sat and watched in painful recognition, self-conscious, and unsure where to stuff all the feelings. The room was hot and small and there was nowhere to go. When the mime was over, they bowed and then embraced one another, oblivious for a moment to the rest of us. We didn't clap, though we wanted to.

They pulled up stools to join our circle and we sat contemplating, in no hurry to fill the void. After a while, I suggested our hosts might like to begin the conversation by asking us some questions. One of the workers, tousle-haired with ruddy skin and a broken tooth in his smile, had a question.

"I know you are business people," he said. "I know you are investors. And I want to know, how do you treat the workers in your factories?"

Startled, the group looked from one to another, seeking a volunteer to respond. Their eyes fell on one of the two Chinese investors amongst them who nodded his assent. He looked around as he considered what to say.

The man (I shall call him Yan) paused for a while, then lowered his head to look at the floor. There was a long silence and then he lifted his face to stare at the ceiling, breathing deeply. Finally, with a loud rasp from deep in his gut, and an upward heave of his shoulders, he began to sob. We sat together for minutes that felt like hours, as all the emotion flowed out. His colleagues looked embarrassed, shifting on their stools and struggling to look at him or at anyone else. The room felt stifling and somehow electric. Eventually one of the migrants, a tiny young woman, stood up, drew a handkerchief from her pocket and gave it to the weeping man. Another did the same, whilst we sat still and did nothing.

After a while the crying subsided. Yan said he was ready to speak, but that first, he wished to address our hosts in Chinese. They nodded and he began. His words clearly resonated as they sat watching him closely. When he was finished, my colleague Lanying nodded slowly and offered to speak on Yan's behalf, translating what he'd said into English, so that he wouldn't have to repeat himself.

"I am deeply sorry for the way you live and the way you're treated," he said. "I know what you've shown us is true. I've seen it for myself many times. I hope that I'm not a part of this, that my company is not a part of this. But I also know in my heart that in some way we are all responsible. I know this is about all of us. I want to understand my role, through what I've done and what I've not done, and what I've chosen not to see.

"My greatest fear for the Chinese people is that we will split apart and break. I fear we will fail to speak to one another and to hear one another – that we will lose our harmony. I fear that we will let the gap widen and that it will consume us. I want to thank you for meeting us today – for truly meeting us. I am deeply grateful and I will never forget it."

Later, as we left, I turned and looked at the CEO who had asked me the question: "So Lindsay, tell me, how do you measure the impact of what you do?"

I knew he had his answer and so did all his colleagues. Sometimes the most important things in life don't come down to inputs, outputs and metrics. Sometimes they call for a deeper kind of knowing.

"That day changed us, it changed our business," he told me later. "It strengthened us as a team, and forced us to look at our priorities differently. It made us pay attention to issues a few steps away, things we could easily otherwise ignore. I think it was about seeing what was possible, knowing you can break the status quo. Once you know that, there's no good reason not to do it."

Chapter Five
How Much is Enough?

"There will always be another mountain," said Naidu. "You need an inner smile!"

It was early morning and he and I were sitting drinking tea in the shade of a majestic banyan tree in the garden of the Taj West End hotel in Bangalore. We'd finished a Quest the previous night. As we'd hoped, the participants had ended the week excited and re-energised by the experience, but I felt empty and a bit defeated. I was still learning how to give out so much personal energy without draining myself to the point of exhaustion in the process. As usual, I would have to sink into my own world for a while, to go vacant. Only then would I begin to feel my spirit replenish. It was often painful – a crash that I had yet to work out how to soften.

There had been one particular man who'd found the week a struggle. He'd had a furious outburst with me, unhappy to feel confronted by the world he was witnessing. It was a familiar pattern. I knew that sometimes the things people saw with us triggered strong reactions. I'd sat late into the previous evening, talking with him until at some point, something had shifted and he'd found himself in a better place. It was like watching a big fish swimming in a small pond of its own making, with the banks piled high to keep the ocean out. The biggest fish were usually powerful people, and because they had more power, they felt they had more to lose than everyone else, more to protect. I knew what it had taken to get to where they were, because in some ways I was the same. I could see them holding it all together, could feel the fear.

Here with Naidu, in the cool of the garden, I sat and let go of some of my own drive – to do more, to be more. I thought about all we'd achieved in the previous days, and about one of my own recurring questions. How much is enough? I sat with Naidu reflecting on my own ambition, and it appeared somehow ridiculous in a funny, valiant sort of way. We spoke of the impulse to do what we felt was right, even when it seemed pointless, and the beauty of the small act rather than the grand gesture. Naidu's work, with the mentally ill and their families, was about helping people who went largely unseen. He'd learned to persevere in situations where the need was limitless.

"Just smile, Lindsay," he laughed. "Smile to yourself! Isn't one life changed worth your while?"

I decided to share with Naidu how my week had started, in Delhi just six days earlier.

"I went back to see a woman named Shakeela," I told him. "I met her last year on a visit with Sanjay when she was in the midst of a terrible crisis. I'm sorry to say I haven't changed her life, Naidu, at least not in any sort of helpful way. But she's made an impression on mine and I'm still wondering what to make of it. I'd like to tell you about her. The story goes back to our first encounter a year ago."

~

"Please come," Sanjay had said. "They're expecting us and I promised you'd come. It's important because it will help you understand. But it's very challenging."

After what we'd already witnessed that evening, it was difficult to imagine how much more challenging it could be.

"OK," I said. "We'll come."

It was very late and we were all exhausted, but Sanjay and Paramjeet had asked that we make one final stop with them. There were some people they were working with, whom they wanted to introduce us to, and so we made the journey across town, bouncing about in the back of yet another minibus. It was 2008 and I was travelling with a small group of participants, all of them part of a Quest to India. One of the men, a hedge fund manager from London, kept asking what Sanjay and Paramjeet were doing to get the people we were on our way to meet into school and jobs and on their way up the ladder to a better life. I knew this was the wrong question, but it wasn't easy to explain why.

The driver pulled up next to an extended, shapeless, wild patch of shrubs and yellow-green grass at a chaotic intersection – more of a large traffic roundabout than the small park it was meant to be. Cars, taxis, three wheelers, buses and trucks went whizzing by, tooting, blaring and screeching, with no apparent pattern to their flow.

"I'm so sorry about the traffic," said Sanjay as if it were a surprise. "It's really crazy! Please be careful. Try not to get hit!"

We climbed out of the minibus and were swept up into the full force of a stream of people, ducking and weaving expertly through the cars, swift and intense, as they went about their evening's business. Half running to keep up, we followed Sanjay and Paramjeet, and headed for the snaking spirals of smoke that marked countless homeless families, huddled around makeshift pavement fires. Thin, shadowy figures moved to and fro in the half light. Passing through a broken gate and into a scrub-land park, we could make out ramshackle clumps of people, dishevelled and without shelter. This was home, and they were preparing for another night camped out in Delhi's pungent, cold air.

Dimly, people of all ages began to appear, until a crowd of about a hundred had gathered round us and Sanjay was in full flight, talking, joking and telling little stories to convey a sense of who we were and why we'd come to visit. The crowd were full of questions, most of which he couldn't answer, about the police who beat them up last week and the disgruntled local residents who wanted them gone.

These were families of all generations. One baby was just three days old. They had lived in the vicinity for forty years, having originally migrated from Maharashtra State to the south. Many had been born here on this park-cum-traffic roundabout and many had died here also. Their previous home was about a hundred yards away, but in its place there now stood a three star hotel, its light spilling out across the park. They'd been moved on by the police a few years back – no one knew how long ago – and ended up here.

We stood and talked, trying to absorb an unfamiliar world. I felt a tug at the foot of my jeans. I looked down to find a young woman, propped up in the dark and the dirt, hair wild, eyes piercing, wide and frightened. She was squatting on one foot, and supporting herself from behind with her elbows, whilst her other leg stuck up skywards, newly severed above the knee, white bone and red raw flesh and covered with a thin transparent bandage.

In shock, I dropped down beside her on the ground. She was small and child-like and she looked confused, like someone whose life had just slipped out of her own hands.

"Who is she?" I was almost shouting. "Look, she's lost her leg! Where are her family?"

As Sanjay took in the scene an animated discussion began and a minute or two later came the response.

"Her name is Shakeela. She was hit by a truck yesterday. She has six children and they live here with her. There is no one else."

The people with me looked on aghast and visibly distressed. The scene was so far beyond anything they might have imagined. It felt extraordinary and yet, from the responses of those around us, it seemed that such an accident was commonplace. I sensed no lack of care, but rather, continuous adaptation to harsh circumstance. For my part, I felt sick to the stomach and wanted to do something practical, to offer to pay hospital bills or whatever else was required, but it felt like a hopeless gesture. They didn't need our help and it wouldn't really change a thing. We'd crossed paths with Shakeela at a moment of crisis in her life, the ramifications of which she and her family would live with forever. But the context was so extreme that I could find no decent response. The conversation with the community ran on. Shakeela had been to the hospital. There was nothing more to be done. This was how life was here.

Later, as we took our leave and returned, very subdued, to our hotel, we spoke together about what the evening had meant for each of us, how to begin to make sense of it. For me, it felt like another stark moment when the brutality of life was right there in front of my face. How to be useful? This lingering question went beyond the immediate situation and a fleeting relationship with a young woman in distress. It was about the difference between standing by and stepping up to something more. It was about finding new ways to be effective, without being consumed by the depth and scale of problems to which there were no adequate answers.

~

It's 2009. I follow Shakeela's slow and partial recovery until I am back in Delhi and then I arrange to see her again. Sanjay organises the meeting. It will take place under the twinkling lights of New Delhi's ceremonial boulevard, Rajpath, just a mile or so away from Shakeela's roadside home. She arrives by taxi as a smoky twilight falls, accompanied by Mr Singh and Mr Shastri, two gentlemen volunteer workers from the homeless community. We find a place beneath a tree in the lengthening shadow of India Gate, and sit down together on the grass to talk. Mr Shastri, his tunic sharply pressed and a little cap on his head, offers to translate. Shakeela is dressed in a worn, pink shalwar khameez and a black shawl, her imaginary leg tucked habitually beneath her. She smiles shyly in recognition.

"I've often thought about you since our meeting a year back," I say. "I've been worried about whether you're coping and hoping for the best. I'd like to know how you're getting along."

"I remember you," she replies, looking at me steadily. "I remember the night you came to visit."

"I'm interested to know more about your life Shakeela," I respond. "I wonder if you'd be willing to tell me your story?"

She nods slowly and folds her hands together in her lap. "Yes," she replies. "I am happy to tell it."

Shakeela is dark skinned with a pretty, open face and a tiny bird-like frame. She needs a cataract operation and her left eye is completely glazed over, but the right one is lively and engaged. Since the accident she moves about on her hands and bottom, manoeuvring with her good leg. She shuffles where she needs to and travels only small distances.

"I was born beside the road," she says. "My family had lived in that place for a few years already. They came from our village to look for work and they never went back to their birth place. I didn't go to school or learn to read or write. I got married to a man who also came from the street. I have six children. Two are boys and four are girls. The older two have children of their own now and my youngest was born four years back."

I ask if she knows her age, and how the family make their living.

A little discussion takes off in Hindi about the age question, counting on fingers. "She's around the middle thirties," comes the reply from Mr Shastri.

"We're all in the balloon business – the whole family," says Shakeela, quite proudly. "We sell balloons to people in the passing cars."

"My husband was a good man, a very good man. Just before the birth of my youngest he went back to visit his place of origin in Pune. He went to bathe in a canal but it was a time of high water. He lost his footing and went under and when he came back up he was drowned. So now it's just me and the children, but we take care of one another."

"How have you coped since your accident?" I ask. "It must have changed many things."

"We manage all right. At first they gave me crutches. But then a few months later my little one strayed into the traffic and when I went to catch her, I was hit by a car. Since then my shoulder doesn't work well and I can't use the crutches."

"What about your confidence?" I ask. "How do you feel about yourself today?"

"Oh, I'm learning all the time!" she says looking straight at Mr Shastri and Mr Singh. "I've learned a lot from them. They've helped me think about the future and my children. And look, here I am today, talking with you! I have a voice and you want to know my story."

I tell Shakeela about my husband, David, our own three sons at home in London, and how I came to India by plane. She smiles in the yellow of the street lamps and then begins to laugh, motioning with delicate hands that move like birds flying through the air.

"Tell me," she says. "I think your husband travels all over the world doesn't he? I can imagine you two crossing in the sky. You have very busy lives going here and there and everywhere."

Yes he does, and yes we do, I reply.

"I knew it!" she says happily, clapping her hands together.

"Tell me," I say. "How do you keep going, after all of this? Getting up each morning must be hard. Life has taken a toll."

"Oh no," she replies firmly, a sparkle in her bright eye. "I know why I am here. We're a very close family and my children are my inspiration. I'm here because of them."

I sit there a little dumbfounded in the soft light of Rajpath. I was, at the time, eight years into the Leaders' Quest journey and I could feel another level of vulnerability to crack through. It was as if I was still coming to terms with ever deeper layers of interconnection. I was grateful to be learning so much about life and relationships and, at the same time, the implications appeared daunting. Here was Shakeela, living day by day, entirely in the present, with a resilience I could scarcely imagine. Her life was very hard – harder than any life should be – and yet she found dignity and meaning in it. I thought about happiness and where it comes from. I wondered at the sliver of chance that separates a person with apparent security from another who has almost none. I sat beside Shakeela on the grass, overcome by the gulf between us, and I wanted, more than anything else, to step across the gap and watch it disappear.

~

Our work moved on, and as it did, from time to time an especially interesting request would come our way. Something would fire our imagination and we'd find ourselves saying yes to an unexpected, yet intriguing, new opportunity.

"We're raising a new investment fund for Africa," the boss of a private equity firm said to me over coffee one morning. "We'd like to take some of our biggest investors to Nigeria, to see what it's like on the ground. We want to help them understand the social and political context we have to navigate, as well as the opportunities for business there. How would you feel about putting together a Quest for us in Lagos?"

We agreed to go ahead. In the months that followed, along with Melanie Katzman, one of our partners, I spent many hours researching Nigeria, and then spent a week in Lagos, to get to know people whom we might meet on the forthcoming trip. It was a steep, but fascinating, learning curve, and by the time the Quest came around, we'd assembled a great programme of meetings and visits. The participants came from different financial firms and each of them was responsible for growing the assets entrusted to them by multiple investors. Their clients included wealthy individuals and big institutions, but by far the largest sums came from millions of ordinary people, including teachers, nurses and factory workers, whose pension funds they managed.

We all arrived for the start of the programme on a late night flight from Johannesburg, to spend two ill-tempered hours swatting huge mosquitoes as we waited to get through immigration. It was a process apparently designed to lower expectations well before anyone formally arrived into the country. Eventually, we emerged from the airport building to be met by a minibus and two heavy duty Jeeps with four security outriders on each. They were all armed with machine guns and wore dark glasses, despite the fact that it was almost pitch black. The drive to downtown Lagos was notorious for hold-ups and we had agreed to follow our hosts' advice and travel with a security escort on the airport road. I thought we were probably more at risk from the security men than from any outside threat, but we stuck to the advice we'd been given and set off in convoy, with the Jeep drivers flashing their headlights and ostentatiously hooting their horns. An hour or so later, we arrived at the hotel and were checking in, when a power cut struck and all the lights went out. There was nothing for it but to decamp to the garden for a beer.

Our itinerary was a fascinating one, and over the next few days, we met with government ministers, journalists and with leaders of businesses large and small. We discussed inflation, corruption, the legal system and social change. We spent time with senior executives from one of the major oil multinationals producing oil in the Niger Delta (and accused of environmental destruction and complicity with a corrupt government), as well as with one of the NGOs that opposed them. We even visited a business which manufactured foam mattresses for the domestic market. In a part of the world where most people had yet to sleep on a bed, the mattress business was a great one to be in. Many things about the week stood out. But for me, and I suspect for most of the group, the most impactful experience took place in a slum named Makoko, which sat at the edge of the Lagos lagoon.

The night before the visit, we dined with a senior government minister who spoke about his party's vision for the future of the country and responded with ease and charm to sceptical questions about its record to date. Over dessert, his wife, who was dressed in a magnificent colourful costume, asked me what we had planned for the following day.

"We're going to Makoko with the leaders of a local NGO," I told her.

"Oh, I've never been there," she replied. "But I'd love to go."

"Come with us!" I said. It seemed too good an opportunity to miss, the chance to show the wife of one of the country's leaders something of life in one of its poorest quarters. Still, I was surprised when she said yes.

"You need to come incognito," I said. "No security people or anything, you just come as one of us. Can you meet us at the hotel at eight tomorrow morning?"

The next day, I found the minister's wife waiting in the lobby, fifteen minutes ahead of the agreed time, dressed in jeans, a loose shirt, headscarf and sunglasses. I hadn't expected her to turn up. Waiting there with me as the group assembled, was a man named Peter Ngomo. He was the Director of an NGO called Healthmatters, which delivered holistic programmes to improve the health of communities in some of the city's most deprived areas. Peter had a cheerful, open face and wore frameless spectacles, suspended from a bright and multi-coloured bead chain round his neck.

Just after eight o'clock, we climbed into a minibus and set off for Makoko through the teeming, frenetic streets of Lagos – an ocean of people, diving in and out of the traffic, or packed onto two-wheelers like rows of squashed sardines. There were vehicles of every description, from smart four-wheel drives that honked in vain in near-stationary traffic, to beaten up, patchwork cars that hung together haphazardly, exhausts belching. Everywhere was a mash of colour, street signs, posters and graffiti, vibrant with street kids, vendors, police and security out-riders – all of them part of a complex urban ecosystem, chaotic and pulsating with life.

An apprehensive quiet settled on our group as Peter began to explain his work. He told us that Healthmatters focused on women and children, providing basic healthcare, and helping women into livelihoods so they could support their children and avoid falling into debt. It also operated micro lending schemes, designed to help poor families lift themselves out of poverty. As we travelled along ever-rougher roads, the surrounding homes became more wretched, and the mud and waste increasingly impenetrable. When our minibus could go no further, we pulled up and got out to walk. Peter led the way, turning to us before ducking down a narrow passage to say, not unkindly, "Some of what you will see may shock you, but this is how life is here."

Makoko is one of those places where people seem to be on the edge of existence. A packed and overflowing slum, it sits on sodden landfill comprised entirely of household waste, and extends far out into the Lagos lagoon. Shacks perch precariously on stilts above thick, filthy water, connected by ramshackle pathways of broken planks. It seems absurdly easy to fall in, and no doubt many people do. I found it difficult to imagine surviving even a few days here – let alone starting a micro business.

The day disappeared in a dizzying array of people and experiences. We visited a mobile healthcare unit parked on the edge of the slum, treating patients as they came in off the street. We met women's groups developing micro lending schemes to set themselves up as street vendors and support their families. We made our way carefully down narrow alleyways and across splintered planks over the lagoon, pausing to speak to people who carried their day's business in brightly coloured bundles on their heads. We met the local priest, stout and well-fed in his long white robes and heavy crucifix, then visited a school, suspended, dark and dirty just above the water line, where a single teacher struggled defiantly in the gloom, a hundred children clustered at his feet. We stopped to witness sewing classes and typing lessons on antique typewriters, all taking place in tiny spaces and near-boiling temperatures.

We saw the efforts of people on the fringes of society, eager to equip themselves with whatever skills they could. Dripping with sweat, submerged in a kind of numb daze as the temperature soared past 40°C, we exchanged greetings with dignified local chieftains in the cramped homes that people opened up to us, and responded bravely to speeches of welcome with our own greetings. We were physically uncomfortable, of course, but that was the least of it.

As the afternoon came to a close, we said our thank-yous and goodbyes, surrounded by a growing crush of people, unused to receiving visitors and curious to carry on talking to us. With difficulty, we squeezed through the crowd, climbed into the minibus and began to pull away. Men and women banged on the windows to catch our attention, while children waved, shouted and pulled funny faces. The bus began to accelerate and I heard an urgent hammering on the rear window. There, with her face pressed up against the glass and a look of total panic in her eyes, was the minister's wife.

"Oh my god!" I said. "We've left her behind!" The driver screeched to a halt, she scrambled to the door, and we hauled her up the steps, while I apologised profusely.

As the group sat together on the drive back to the hotel, it was hard to know what to say. We'd talked with people in Makoko about the menfolk's work as fishermen in the lagoon, the women's job of smoking the day's catch for sale in the city streets, and their desire to educate their children. We'd discussed the struggle to avoid chronic ill health and, in particular, malaria. Here were tens of thousands of people, living inches above stagnant water in an area that was rife with mosquitoes. In the moment, I think we all found it difficult to muster our hope and rise to the dignity and resilience of Peter, his colleagues, and the locals who had welcomed us so warmly.

By the end of the week, we knew that this experience had been as important as any of our conversations with heads of multinationals or government ministers. Our group wanted to invest in Nigeria and earn a profit in the process. They were also willing to confront the complexity and interconnectedness of life on the ground and think about ways that business can transform an economy and the lives of people who depend on it. It wasn't yet clear how these new experiences would translate into imaginative business decisions, and the linkages were far from obvious. What did responsible investment look like in a country like Nigeria? What did it imply for executives running companies here, financial professionals providing capital, or ordinary people all over the world whose savings they were investing? For my part, it would take another visit to Makoko, twelve months later, to really appreciate what the place and its people had to teach me.

~

When I returned the following year, it was with a group of twelve leaders from business, NGOs and civil society. In the intervening months, thanks to the generosity of one of our earlier visitors, Leaders' Quest had provided fifty women with funds to purchase fish smoking equipment, trained them how to start their own fish selling businesses, and helped them to access micro finance loans.

A modest grant of $5,000 had funded a workshop on basic business skills, and provided each of the women with the equipment to get started. Through a revolving loan scheme, they'd each received a sum of $100. The project had already raised productivity and sales, which in turn had enabled them to employ twenty other women from the community. Most of them were supporting eight to twelve family members, so the additional income had directly benefitted around seven hundred people.

Some of the dwellings had recently been demolished by the authorities, and fresh layers of household rubbish had been dumped in the area. As a result, the ground on which we walked was slightly less soggy. Underfoot was a bizarre mosaic of compressed and pounded plastic bottles, crushed cans and discarded carrier bags as far as the eye could see, interspersed with streams and channels of green and brackish lagoon water, where fat black and pink pigs snuffled and swam amidst the muck.

As we made our way through this wasteland, we passed smoking fires laden with small, curled silver fish, brittle scales glinting in the sun, as they cooked gently on the trash in front of someone's home. The women who were guiding us stopped every so often to introduce us to someone who'd gained from the project. The investment in these women, combined with their grit, determination and personal pride had made a difference. They'd taken tiny amounts of loan capital and were using it to sustain themselves and their children at the most basic level. They were desperate for more and eager to demonstrate their success. But it was a difficult journey. I think we all felt deeply troubled, confronted with such extreme poverty.

This disquiet and sense of inadequacy was compounded as the afternoon came to a close, and we gathered in a makeshift community space to say our farewells. All the women who had benefitted from the equipment were there. They were appreciative – which of course was not the point – but many were also evidently worn down, their spark low, and somehow the atmosphere felt incredibly oppressive. One of them stepped forward and all the women lowered their heads and knelt on the floor. Confused, I asked Peter what it meant.

"They are saying thank you," he said.

My heart sank and I felt humiliated. I thanked them for the time we'd spent with them, but the words felt totally inadequate. The edge of this lagoon was the front of a tidal wave of need and injustice and for a while I felt swamped by it. I wanted to meet these women on confident ground but I couldn't find it. I think they knew this, but still the bridge of understanding between us felt shaky. How to stay in the room, look someone in the eye, and say you can't help? And anyway, why can't you?

Sometimes, I think one has to simply dwell with what is and let it settle in the heart. I so wanted to rise to the occasion that afternoon – for the women fish smokers, for the Quest participants, for myself. I wanted to step across my own distress and show my appreciation to these women for being here with us, to be present in a way that fully acknowledged who they were. But I couldn't. I think I felt shame for the yawning gap between us, rage at the inequity of it all, and fear at the precariousness of life.

Over dinner that evening, we spoke about our day and what it meant to each of us. I was reminded of Brené Brown's idea[2] that, in different ways, we are all struggling with our emotions and that the most significant of these is shame, stemming not from guilt – we haven't necessarily done anything wrong – but rather from empathy. My experience that day was about seeing people who were part of the same human family, living in degrading conditions and effectively excluded from mainstream society. It was about shared identity and crossing the silence and the awkwardness which often shrouds these very difficult issues: dignity, inequality, the worth of a person.

There was more too. I realised that in the midst of my own feelings, I'd missed the beauty of the day. I'd missed the energy and spirit of people striving to build a future in a community teeming with enterprise. I'd missed Peter's belief in each and every one of them – the women in the micro finance scheme, the children bursting with life – and his own quiet confidence, born of experience, that they could take an opportunity and turn it into something promising.

Chapter Six
Salaam, Shalom

I n parallel to my work with Leaders' Quest, my personal life continued to be full. David and I were each regularly invited to get involved in different initiatives and, mostly, we had to turn them down for lack of time. A notable exception for both of us, however, had arrived way back in 2002 in the form of an invitation from an irrepressible social entrepreneur named Daniel Lubetzky.

We had first met Daniel in Geneva when he was launching a characteristically bold plan for a new grassroots movement in the Middle East. The purpose of this new organisation, OneVoice, was to help build the foundations for a two-state solution between Israel and Palestine, by mobilising the silent majority of mainstream nationalists on both side of the divide. These were the ordinary citizens, often ignored, who wanted an end to the conflict and wanted to live in peace with their neighbours.

We were intrigued by what he was doing, and over the next few years, what started out as encouragement and a small commitment, expanded until both David and I found ourselves doing far more with Daniel and OneVoice than either of us really had time for. Soon I was devoting several hours a month to the movement and making occasional trips to the Middle East. A European office had taken root in a ground floor room at the Leaders' Quest office in London and we had assembled a board and small staff to work with teams in Ramallah, Gaza, Tel Aviv and New York.

The parallels with Quests were surprisingly strong. They included a willingness to chip away at a large stone, sometimes with very little prospect of shaping it. This kind of work was about painful compromises on both sides – Israeli and Palestinian. It stemmed from the belief that without them (for example on borders, refugees, a shared capital city), there will be no resolution, no long-term security, and a large number of people will continue to live without hope and opportunity.

As one of the "neutral" actors in the camp, from time to time I was asked to facilitate some of the face-to-face meetings between our staff and Youth Councils – especially at the predictable times of turmoil that occur in the region with depressing regularity, in response to death and destruction on one side or the other.

One such moment came at the beginning of 2009, in the aftermath of the Gaza War. The preceding months had seen an escalation in tension, culminating in the collapse of an uneasy truce between Israel and Hamas, the organisation that governed the coastal enclave. Around thirteen hundred Palestinians and thirteen Israelis had been killed during the three weeks of fighting.

As a result, communication between our teams had deteriorated to an all-time low. People were in despair, incensed with one another and depressed at what had unfolded. The OneVoice Gaza office, under threat from Hamas for espousing a two-state solution (and for supporting the right of Israel to exist, which Hamas did not), and under fire from the Israeli incursion, had been forced to close. One of our supporters had lost thirteen family members, including nine children, in an Israeli air strike on Gaza, and many Israeli supporters had been called up for military service in the conflict.

Shortly after the war ended, we brought together our leadership teams from both sides – about twenty five people in all – for two days of meetings in the Ambassador Hotel in East Jerusalem. My role was to facilitate and help them figure out a way forward.

The first day got off to a miserable start. One of the most important Palestinian team members, Abdullah, who ran our Youth Leadership programme, was absent, unable to secure a permit from the Israeli Defence Force to cross from the West Bank. Others arrived late, delayed in queues at checkpoints, all part of an endless, tedious process, humiliating for everyone involved. Resentment bubbled in the room before we even began. On one side, fury at the brutality and scale of destruction and loss of life inflicted, on the other an angry despair at fighting a war most had no appetite for, but believed to be necessary.

Two different narratives poured out, long, historic, bitter and frustrated. Neither side could look the other in the face nor hear anything they had to say. They had no interest in really listening. They already knew it all. The conflicting stories were too hard-wired, the wounds and disappointments too deep.

The first few hours felt like a complete waste of time. The atmosphere was tense, sullen and suspicious, fuelled by numerous impromptu breaks for coffee and cigarettes because people simply had to escape one another. Frustrated with the stalling and the repetition, I asked the two teams to separate and work out what they were willing to do, to help their colleagues on the other side move forward. I wanted them to focus on the actions they could take that would build trust with one another, rather than continue endlessly advancing their own agenda. There were clearly compromises we needed to find within our own organisation – never mind those we were demanding from the respective political leaders – if we were to have any kind of future.

In the break that followed, I went from room to room and it became clear that the Palestinian team were getting ready to be bold and move on some of the issues that had long held the organisation in deadlock. As we reassembled, I tried to persuade them to speak first, to set the scene, but they refused and so it fell to the Israeli team to begin.

They did a disastrous job. They gave nothing and seemed to lack empathy, unaware of the huge disappointment and raw anger their words engendered. Probably, they were embarrassed and had nowhere to go, having failed to reach agreement amongst themselves in the hours before. The Palestinians looked on, furious and vindicated by what they saw as business as usual. Daniel was deeply disappointed and angry and I lost my patience with him in a futile and counter-productive attempt to get us back on track. It almost felt like a black comedy.

I turned to Nisreen, the leader of the Palestinian staff, and asked if she would stand up and convey to the group what her team had prepared, unchanged and unabridged. Eventually, she agreed. She stood looking very solemn while, through clenched teeth, she spat out a brave and generous speech.

"We know what we need to do to prove to Israelis that you have a partner for peace on the other side. We understand that you need to be able to show Israelis that we are talking in the Palestinian street about the things we have to give up to achieve peace, as well as what we have to gain. We know it's about building mutual trust, addressing the deepest fears of the other. For you it is loss of security, an existential fear. For us it is that we will never have a state, fear that you will never deliver."

The Israelis looked miserable. One of them was crying and others simply shook their heads, cornered, outplayed, or maybe just very weary. It was way past lunchtime. We'd prepared some long tables in the dining room for everyone to sit together and eat hummus. Clearly that wasn't going to work.

"Can you please split the seating up?" I said to the waiters. "We need two tables now, as far apart as possible."

The Israeli team spent the meal with their heads down in deep discussion, barely touching the food. As we re-gathered after lunch, one of them came to speak to me.

"We want to start again. We want to wipe out what we said earlier. We'd like to be the first to speak."

The team leader stood up, earnest and serious, and spoke directly to Nisreen, looked her in the eye, and found the common ground to say what needed to be said.

"We trust you and you can trust us. We're willing to work as partners, we know the message we need to take to our streets. We'll say what needs to be said, even if our own people don't want to hear it."

People began to speak from a deeper place. Passion, anger and tears flowed, but the rhetoric stopped. Counterparts held each other's gaze even though it was deeply uncomfortable to do so. Individuals physically turned to look at one another, their own fear and regret, impossible to check, silently playing out as they listened to someone else's story.

It had taken the whole of the first day to work out just how bad our situation was. We had very little we agreed upon. We didn't agree on what was violence and what was non-violence. One person's war is another person's fight for freedom. We didn't agree on what was extremist behaviour and what was moderate. One person's extremist is another person's soldier. The choice to stay in the room was a difficult one. There was a further choice on offer, to give up on each other and get up and leave. But no one took it.

Somewhere in the middle of a gruelling day, everyone present decided they wanted to stay and be part of the solution. We set to work, deciding programmes for the coming months, agreeing the core messages that each team would push forward in town halls and campuses and across their youth leadership teams. These were people who wanted to believe in each other, leaders willing to go against the consensus in their own societies. The gap between them, and those unprepared to do so, looked like a chasm. So much was stacked against progress. There were so many reasons to let everyone stew in their own pot. But the hope was in the detail. Here, in one room, in one city, we had made progress of sorts – a hard won, tiny microcosm of the whole.

~

Ten months later I was asked to go back. There had been political changes on the ground, a new president in America, escalating tensions with Iran, but ultimately no real progress on the central conflict between the Israelis and Palestinians. The OneVoice teams were back at work, but the scale of the effort needed still felt daunting and the challenge of overcoming disillusion and apathy in Israel, and anger and despair in Palestine, weighed heavily.

I was travelling with three colleagues, John Lyndon and Sayyeda Salaam from London and Darya Shaikh, based in New York. Together with John, Darya carried overall responsibility for the coordination of work on the ground, making frequent trips in and out of the region. Born to a Jewish Israeli mother and a Pakistani Muslim father, Darya had an ideal birthright for her role. John was the perfect ally. An Irish Catholic, he had grown up in a nationalist family in the shadow of the Northern Ireland conflict. He could easily have imagined himself slipping into violence as a teenager.

The main meeting of our visit took place in Beit Jala, an Arab town adjacent to Bethlehem on the West Bank, but under Israeli military control. This was not a place most Israelis chose to visit and to some it felt like hostile territory. But for the Palestinians it meant they could get there without the usual hassle of obtaining permits to cross the border. Importantly, it also meant that Abdullah, leader of our Palestinian youth programme, could be there.

We met in an oversized room in a dislocated hotel, stranded in a lunar landscape. Outside was a terrace where a rare and bitter winter wind was blowing up a noisy storm. We had about thirty people present, including many of the youth leader activists with whom we worked, roughly half from each community, plus Darya, John, Sayyeda and me. For many of those with us, this was one of only a handful of times that they had met directly with the other side without a machine gun or barrier between them.

We made a circle of chairs in the middle of the room for everyone to sit. On a side table stood a couple of urns brewing thick, stewed coffee, a stack of plastic cups and plates of biscuits. After brief introductions, I asked half of those present, the Palestinians and a couple of the international staff, to stand up and form a line. They looked suspicious, unsure where this was going, but did so anyway. I asked the Israelis to stand up and form another line, face to face with the Palestinians and just a few inches apart. And then I asked them each to speak to whomever was standing opposite them, about a person they deeply admired and why. They might be alive or dead, known to them or not: someone who meant something special to them. Every few minutes each person moved along the line to talk to a new partner. The conversations took off, in English for the most part, some of it fluent, some broken. Eyes locked and the energy flowed. People laughed, surprised and curious. I caught sight of Abdullah. He was the tallest person in the room by several inches, a forceful presence with his distinctive shaven head, and he was talking intently with one of the Israelis in broken Hebrew, shoulders bent to listen.

Afterwards we talked about what they had learned about one another: that mothers are hugely important in Palestine, and grandmothers too, and that common ground appears so easily, in a love of movies, or a passion for sport. One Israeli man told how he was looking for the right girl to marry and had found himself speaking to one of his Palestinian counterparts in the same situation. Neither had a family yet, but both dreamt of doing so. They wanted their children to grow up safely and in peace.

Good news followed. The key negotiators of the OneVoice Joint Message had stayed up for much of the previous night to agree the final wording. Three words had been added, and they had succeeded in producing a text both sides could agree upon, after ten months of tricky negotiations. The "Mission and Guiding Principles" at the top of the document were read out by one of the youth leaders, Ahmad, and his Israeli counterpart Guy, and as they finished, the room broke into applause.

Later, Guy spoke about their joint and modest commitment – achieved outside the fraught political process and negotiations that would be needed to achieve peace at the international level.

"We know that OneVoice Israel is only legitimate because OneVoice Palestine exists," he said. "Without a partner on the other side, we're nothing. We needed to find words that enabled our partners to succeed, and they knew we needed the same. It was very tough. We spent many hours on single words. And we learned what matters to them and why, how their story differs from our own. It's been very satisfying ..."

With the Joint Message behind us, the day continued to unfold, interspersed with frequent smoking breaks to congregate on the freezing terrace to shout over the sound of the wind and inhale lungfuls of tobacco. We broke into small, mixed groups to respond to different questions: what do you need to do for us, and we for you? We explored programmes for the coming year and calmly, but passionately, discussed some of the most controversial and sensitive subjects surrounding the conflict.

By the end of the day, it felt as if we were moving. I looked about me at the talented people in the room. There was Ahmad who had been a relentless source of energy and inspiration, sensitive, encouraging, bridging gaps without losing touch with what he stood for; and Guy, quietly thoughtful and articulate, debating his future as an IT expert in Israel, or the alternative of changing course and following a different line of study. There was Antwan, a passionate and articulate youth leader from Bethlehem, who had just been asked to leave his job monitoring settlement growth, because his employers were against his work with us, and the principle of co-operating with Israelis. Yet he remained so cheerful. "I'll find another job," he told me with a smile.

We closed with a circle and each person took a turn to speak. There was cautious optimism, an insistence that this should lead somewhere and be backed up by action, but also hesitancy in the face of so many earlier defeats. There was a strong desire to continue to meet regularly, an almost desperate plea to stay connected and to quietly keep the channels of personal communication open.

"How can we understand one another if we never speak or meet?" someone asked.

I was reminded just how effective the years of keeping people apart had been in fuelling this conflict. Palestinians were accused of "normalisation" (something akin to appeasement or collaboration) for engaging in dialogue with Israelis. The Israelis themselves were prone to alarming generalisations and stereotypes, fearful of the "terrorists" on the other side and far more easily able to insulate themselves from the daily trials and humiliations of this long running confrontation.

Ari, an observant Jew, recently arrived from Poland, spoke up in the circle. "I am very pleased to be here and to have met my cousins," he said.

There was nervous laughter as the resonance sunk in. They were, of course, cousins. We all are. In many ways, this was just a very old family feud spun wildly out of control. And I too had my own small breakthrough. The previous day in our office in Ramallah I'd had a harsh encounter with Abdullah. He was pushing to oust the man who led the office there, believing he should take his place. I'd told him it was not an option and we'd argued. In one of the smoking breaks I sought him out. He was visibly pleased with the day and surprised by the outcomes and the open dialogue. I wanted to speak to him privately and I pulled aside another colleague, Ezz, to help us translate. Abdullah spoke very little English and I spoke no Arabic.

"I'm sorry we had such a tough conversation yesterday, Abdullah," I said. "I didn't want to be rude or disrespectful, and I'm sorry if I sounded so."

Abdullah took my hand, shaking his head slowly and looked me intently in the eye.

"I didn't know you," he said. "I didn't understand who you are. Now, today, I know. I recognise you, and I'm pleased to work with you."

I smiled inside and out. This was someone who'd chosen to swim against the tide and make room to hear the other. Yet he remained deeply loyal to his own cause.

"I'd like to come back to see you if I may, Abdullah," I said. "I'd like to know more about you and why you do what you do."

We agreed on a plan. I wasn't sure when, but I would return to visit him. I had the impression that Abdullah had some special qualities, and I wanted to learn more about who he was.

~

"He smokes like an old oven," said Ezz without irony. "Where he comes from in Yabad, they're tobacco farmers. He thinks if he quits smoking they'll take away his citizenship."

It was mid-afternoon on the sixteenth day of Ramadan and eighteen months since my last visit to the West Bank. I was travelling with my fourteen year old son, Joe, and we had come to visit Abdullah and to hear his story. Joe and I had arrived at Israel's Ben Gurion airport earlier that day, and taken a taxi to Ramallah. It had been a straightforward drive, passing a long queue of traffic crawling in the opposite direction, as we crossed the checkpoint into the West Bank without delay.

Abdullah was waiting for us, dressed in a chocolate-coloured T-shirt and loose jeans, when we pulled up, He wore a newly-minted, thick silver wedding band on his left hand. He greeted us with strong handshakes and a curt nod of his head, swiftly identifying Joe with the Arabic – and Hebrew – pronunciation of his name – Yousef. Abdullah had been married a few weeks back and had just returned from honeymoon. As we walked inside I asked him how he was finding his new life. He shook his head and let out a long breath.

"Ouuff, it's difficult, very difficult," he said. "After fifteen years on my own ... now there are two of us, me and my wife ..." He trailed off gesturing with his hands to signal the flow of time and a bend in the river.

Across the city almost everyone was fasting, locked into the rhythm of an annual rite, a couple of hours away from breaking the day's fast with a meal. We were nearing the end of the hottest summer the region had ever recorded and energy levels ebbed and flowed in the sweltering heat.

"It's just a fight within yourself. Personal discipline," said Ezz. "And of course I'm losing weight!"

Sitting together now, Abdullah looked at me across the table, serious and dignified – happy to have a chance to say what he wanted to say. Ezz had agreed to join us, again, to translate.

"My name is Abdullah," he began. "I come from a village. called Yabad, beside Jenin and close to the border between the West Bank and Israel. We are eleven children and I am the youngest. My mother had six girls before the first boy was born, and here, you know, having boys is very important. My father was a tobacco farmer and he passed away when I was two years old. Then when I was six, my mother went to Jordan to fetch one of my sisters and she was killed in a car crash. I lost my parents as teachers, and so I was educated by our neighbours and the community.

"I learned right and wrong from them, how we judge one another on the street, why we love this one, and hate that one. I was affected greatly by our neighbours. My sisters emphasised my role as a boy, a man. At a very young age I needed to answer the question: who am I? And what is my role in this life?

"Our financial situation was very bad, so we boys worked, usually packing coal, which is an important industry in Yabad. In the first Intifada, my brother Ahmad was very active and he was arrested by the Israelis and sent to jail for five years. Another brother, Mohammad, went to Jordan to study and then to India, where he stayed. That left me as the head of the household at fourteen. Whether or not I had the right qualities, leadership fell to me. So I worked, and when the school was open, I studied. Our school overlooked a settlement and daily we would throw stones. Often the Israelis closed it because of this, and so for many months we had no lessons. My education was very patchy and never really complete.

"Being so close to the settlements, many of us worked there and some became fluent in Hebrew. By day I worked constructing the buildings of the occupiers, and by night I would gather with my friends to throw stones at them. The settlers are our enemies. They took our lands and we have all heard the stories of the generations before us who lost their homeland. Throwing stones was a payback for the wrong done to our families, a form of resistance against the occupier. This went on for two or three years, but I began to realise it wasn't a good life. By day, the man I was working for would say to me, 'I think I saw you last night, wearing

84

a yellow T-shirt. Why were you throwing stones at us?'

"In the evenings, we'd gather and drink coffee and speak of resistance, discussing and discussing. The leader was a guy with many kids and he too worked in the settlements. He'd been in prison and was very patriotic and nationalistic, urging us to action. One evening we had a very hard discussion. I asked him, 'Why do we work for them by day and throw stones at night? It's wrong that we are building their cities for them.'

"'We have no other option,' he replied. 'We need to work there to earn money and feed our families.'

"'There is another choice,' I said. 'We can stay here and work for less pay in our own country and we can build our state.' And then I walked out of the meeting and the next day I left my job and continued to think about what I could do.

"We hated the Israelis as much as fire hates water. But then came Oslo, 1994, and we watched Abu Ammar [Palestinian President Yasser Arafat] shake hands on television with Rabin [Israeli Prime Minister]. He was the father of our movement, our leader who we were duty bound to follow, and it was very hard to understand what he had done. This affected our thoughts, changed them. I realised that a leader can change direction like day changes to night and have great impact with this choice.

"Life moved on. Many prisoners were released including Ahmad. He went to work in the PLO [Palestinian Liberation Organisation] and, in time, an opportunity came for me to have an interview with a government minister. He was looking for a bodyguard and even though I knew nothing about it, I had the physique for it. The most important thing is that you look the part, so I got the job and they sent me for three months training to learn about weapons and security. I became his shadow. My job put me very close to the leadership, to Arafat and others, and I watched and learned from what they said and did.

"I learned how hard it is for a leader to take a decision that people don't like, and yet which he knows to be the right choice. I learned that being responsible is more important than emotion. That sometimes the street might not approve, yet you must still take the right decision. I looked at Palestinian life and I thought: this is like a soccer game. We have the pitch, we have the ball, the crowd, the team. But we have no goal. We just run round and round ourselves. And I knew that I was one of those people out there on the field, sweating in vain.

"We were far away from identifying an objective and there was a deep sense of despair. So we began the second Intifada, which was the worst decision the leadership could have made, in my opinion. I had friends who died and others who went to prison and all of them I really honour and respect. But it felt to me like a fire that was eating people up, consuming us all. There was great violence with no positive results. Palestinians became terrorists in the eyes of the world and radical elements gained strength and multiplied. In a state of fear, more and more people resort to religion. If you are afraid to die, you'd rather die a believer.

"Life became impossible. I would have to pass through thirty checkpoints, take all my clothes off, go through the valley and across mountains just to move from Yabad to Ramallah. And this was the time when I heard about OneVoice. They offered me a job and I took it. I met Daniel and thought: what is this crazy Mexican Jew doing this for? I liked him as a man and I wondered: why does he come to this country, where we hate Jews and we hate Israelis? I saw someone with charisma and personality and I saw how much he believed in what he was saying.

"I set about this OneVoice work to grow the notion in the Palestinian mind of what it means to have a state, to build it. My work is to move from village to village, talking about what we have to give up, as well as what we have to gain, persuading people, using all my skills. It's difficult. If I meet a group of twenty there may be two that I can really move. But that's fine with me. They say a bullet that doesn't hit its mark still makes a big bang. It's important that people hear us, even if they don't agree with us.

"And then there came a special experience that made an impact on me. OneVoice started a video campaign where we invited Israelis and Palestinians to form pairs and exchange videos with one another, talking about our lives and our vision for the future. I was paired up with an Israeli guy called Alon who was a member of Shas [an ultra-conservative religious political party]. He was about my age and had six children, a religious guy, extremist and no one would agree to pair up with him. But I said, 'I want to work with this person.'

"It was a big challenge. I made my first video with pictures of our house, our land, our way of life and I sent if off to him. His cassette came back and it simply said, 'The house and the land you call yours belongs to me and my children.'

"Daniel was there and he said, 'Let's remove this guy from the programme. He's crazy.' But I said, no, that I wanted to continue. I told Daniel, 'I don't need to convince someone who is already convinced. I need to convince someone who is a blocker, an opposer,' and so I continued to exchange videos with Alon.

"He saw Palestinians as terrorists, killers, but we began to have an interesting conversation, sending videos to and fro. The plan was that after six months each pair should arrange to meet face to face for the first time, in Jerusalem. The idea was that I would get a permit to go into West Jerusalem and he would welcome me and meet me there at the YMCA. Others who had formed pairs were meeting on the beach, going to a bar, falling in love with one another. Daniel said 'We can leave all the love birds to it! Let's concentrate on this one!'

"But then, Alon discovered that the YMCA is a Christian organisation, with crosses and Jesus figures inside and he refused to go. He said that as a religious Jew he would not meet in such a place, but instead would meet me in East Jerusalem and welcome me there.

"I refused. This was to be my first opportunity to see the capital, to visit West Jerusalem, at the age of thirty two. To meet in our land – in occupied East Jerusalem – to be welcomed there by an Israeli, would be to deny it was occupied land. Eventually we were both persuaded, on the condition that I should welcome him. We met at the Ambassador Hotel. His English was as bad as mine. I speak only a little Hebrew and he speaks no Arabic, so we had an interpreter. Alon wouldn't shake my hand and we sat at a table facing one another. We began a dialogue and I said to him, 'My father, my grandfather, all my family come from this place. You cannot cancel our presence based on ancient history. If you want history, I can dig up thousands of years of it too.'

"My aim was to talk to him not about religion but about humanity. I spoke about his children and the children I hope to have one day. I said to him, 'Your kids do not need to live in fear like you do, afraid to travel on the bus. I should be able to move about from place to place freely and to feel secure. We should not pass onto our kids the cycle of violence and centuries of conflict.'

"As we talked and we looked at one another I felt he began to acknowledge me. To see that, yes, the Palestinians are here, and they too have rights, however painful that might be for him to know. I said to him, 'I don't want more than this from you. Your children will move further than you have and believe in the other side. Mine will do the same. Future generations will be able to live in peace as neighbours.'

"I left that meeting convinced that I should work harder and target people who are far away, who reject the notion of peace. It's a big challenge talking to my own people about what it will take. It's a very difficult message and often the whole crowd is against you. But it's the work that needs to be done."

As the sun began to set, we left the office together to go to Iftar – the breaking of the fast – at a local restaurant. The traffic was dense and chaotic and came to a complete standstill as someone tried to turn 180 degrees in the middle of a jam-packed road.

"Their blood sugar is low," explained Ezz, tapping his fingers on the dashboard. "Everyone's hungry and irritable. They want to get home and eat."

Inside the restaurant, food was piled high and the tables were packed with families. Children with heads bent to their plates, women in headscarves, smoking shish pipes with sweet, fruit-scented tobacco. Soup had already been placed on the table, together with the customary dishes of salad – chopped scarlet tomatoes, their pips spilling out in rivulets of juice, fleshy aubergines cooked to a soft pulp and luminous yellow-green pickles. The buffet was laden with baskets of pita bread, still steaming from the oven, and trays of spiced lamb and freshly grilled chicken on skewers. At the far end sat big ceramic painted bowls, piled high with dense and sticky desserts.

Ezz and Abdullah tucked in right away, waving to Joe to fill his plate. It had been a long day. We would resume talking later, but first, we all needed to eat.

~

Three days later, I was across the border in Tel Aviv with my family, for the birthday party of one of our closest friends. The setting was a breathtaking location on a rooftop in the old port of Jaffa. To one side lay the Arab quarter with its elegant curves and courtyards and brick cobbled streets clinging to the hills as they climbed. Rough, gold Jerusalem stone glowed warm and mysterious, reflecting the heat of the day back out into the night. On the other side, spread out before us and spilling into the sea, lay modern Tel Aviv. The city skyline swept the length of a great arc of white sand, catching in the moonlight. Far below, the sound of waves washed back up the hill to echo off the stone.

Here too, the tables were laden with the produce of a fertile land. Fresh, white fish, falling from the bone, diced black olives glistening in oil and the ubiquitous hummus, accompanied by brimming bowls of chopped tomatoes, fat cucumbers, parsley and feta. Known as "Arabic salad" or "Israeli salad", depending who you are and where you come from. Language matters here. It draws the indelible lines that dictate the terms of business, identifying your narrative and your modern day allegiances. It marks the divide between what can and cannot be said, in a land where tension fizzes in the air, enveloping every encounter with nuance.

I felt a sudden urge to run. Like the point in a circle where grief goes full turn and bumps into joy, or the other way round, I couldn't tell the difference between the two, and I didn't need to. I just desperately wanted some peace and space. To be alone and mourn the passage of time and the beautiful, bittersweet intensity of it all.

I ducked out of the party and down the stairs, past a trail of tea-light candles on the steps, and out into the dark. I dropped down the hill to a gap in the pine trees and found a hidden place where I could sit on a low rock wall, look at the sea and let my heart go. I needed to cry and couldn't have stopped if I'd wanted to. I needed to taste the tang of pine, to sense the rapid throb of cricket wings and feel the breeze across my skin, damp with salt.

I sat for a long time on the rock wall and I thought about why I was here, in the Middle East. Abdullah's story was one of tolerance and hope. He understood at some deep level the humanity he shared with people he could easily have dismissed as his enemy. He was willing to trust and to risk being hurt.

I was here with OneVoice for some of the same reasons I was with Leaders' Quest. There were so many lessons to be shared between the two. They were lessons about vision and inclusiveness. There was also something about boundaries and when to let them go – the times when the drive for self-protection blocks the opportunity to really know another person, and in so doing, to learn about yourself.

I knew this from a different context. Half a lifetime ago, at the age of twenty three, I'd fallen irretrievably in love with someone – an Israeli as it happened – and found myself without boundaries. No skin to separate what was on the inside from the universe outside. It shaped me as much as anything ever has, awoke in me empathy and gave me the calm comfort of being seen by someone and not having to explain. Now, I just felt grateful for that first love and the vulnerability it provoked. It simply reaffirmed what I had always known: that I was one tiny fish in a vast ocean; that I didn't live in a pond and I didn't want to.

I had come to the Middle East, in part, to see Abdullah. He was an unlikely hero, pushing his luck, occasionally making things up as he went along, yet with the courage to hold on tight to his own internal compass, and to steer by it. It wasn't certainty or righteousness, but a desire to make good choices. This was the kind of intent that had attracted me to this work in the first place, and would keep me here, despite the frankly dim prospects of overall success. I wasn't about to give up on my own small contribution.

I looked out at the ocean in the light of the shimmering moon. Music and laughter drifted across the cobbles. I longed to stay there all night, with time paused, to relish the intimacy of the dark and the draw of the sea. But I couldn't. There would be people waiting for me and probably looking for me. I stood up and walked across the moonlit street, back to the party, to find my family and friends. It was just after midnight and we danced until 3.00am.

Chapter Seven
William's Web

B ack in South Africa, our relationships continued to build. One of the strongest had been formed with Lesley Ann and some of the prisoners leading change programmes with Khulisa. Following my first visit to Sun City with Lesley Ann, we had returned to meet with the rehab group in the prison's youth wing as part of the upcoming Quest.

It proved to be one of the most moving encounters of the week. It began with an open forum with William and his peers, to explain the initiative they were involved in. We then invited each of the visitors to team up with one or two of the inmates and find their own space in the room to exchange personal stories. The prisoners later told us that this had made them feel encouraged, and in some way seen. They were surprised that people whom they looked upon as serious, would bother to come and spend time with them. They were proud to have the chance to talk about what they were learning and how they were trying to change. The openness that Khulisa had somehow inspired in these men, and the leadership they were now demonstrating within the confines of the prison, were striking. All of them were now leading drug rehabilitation and counselling programmes amongst their peers.

The bridge between our two organisations grew and William emerged as a natural leader. He took an increasingly prominent role, designing workshops with us for subsequent Quests and pushing the limits in terms of what everyone gained from the interactions. As he did so, I saw something in him that was strangely familiar. It was as if his candle burned a little too bright for fear of the dark, and I sensed he would do whatever he could to keep the flame from dying. I liked William. I had faith that he would stick to a positive path, and in the years that followed, whenever I passed through Johannesburg, I tried to stop by and see him.

"He's a good person Lindsay," Lesley Ann said to me on more than one occasion. "If he makes it out of jail alive, he'll have a lot to give."

~

In 2008, Lesley Ann called me to say that William had been given early release.

"He's working in Cape Town," she told me. "I offered him a role with Khulisa, but he wants to move away from everything to do with prison and the kind of work we do. I think you should stay in touch with him, Lindsay. I can imagine him working with you one day."

The idea stuck in the back of my mind and a year or so later, as we prepared another wave of work in Africa, I arranged to stop by and see William. I was curious to know how he was getting on. And if we were ever going to consider offering him work with Leaders' Quest, we would need to know more about his life and how he'd landed up in jail.

When I arrived at the airport in Cape Town, William was waiting for me, the first face I saw at the customs barrier. We headed down to the car park to collect his old Isuzu crew cab and on the drive home we began to talk about life since his release. He told me he'd started his own business, designing, building and operating drilling equipment for construction and mining projects, and he was doing surprisingly well. About a year back, he'd hooked up with Gaylen, the girl he'd left behind when he went to prison. They were planning to get married, but he wasn't sure when. He was in touch with his father, whose health was failing, but had seen his mother only once in the preceding ten years. Her choice, he said.

We arrived home and William introduced me to Gaylen – attractive, auburn-haired and welcoming in a wary sort of way. She was in love, her gaze firmly locked on the future. The next morning, William and I walked the short distance to the sea, past bungalows with bare, short-cropped lawns out front. This was low rise, pick-up truck country, home to tradespeople and their families, self-employed plumbers and builders and small-scale entrepreneurs. In a city spoilt for choice, Blouwberg was just beginning to make its way onto the map, caught somewhere between tired and unremarkable, but with unmistakable promise as a future place to be and with a stunning view across the bay to Table Mountain.

We sat down for breakfast on wooden slatted benches at a seafront café which faced a long, white sandy beach. I was happy to be there. I felt as if I had slipped off the radar for a couple of days and left my watch behind.

"I didn't have friends as a kid," said William. "I was expected to be an adult from a very young age, so I became an adult – grew up very quickly and grew up hard and tough. I was solitary and I became a loner.

"Dad was a driller on construction and mining projects so we moved about all the time, from one site to the next. Mum was very bright and she taught me to read very young. I read like crazy as a kid, books about science, history, democracy, whatever I could get my hands on. But dad was a drinker and violent and, when I was thirteen, my parents got divorced. I got into gangs pretty much right away and I started doing drugs. First marijuana, then ecstasy, LSD, cocaine, heroin, pretty much anything I could find. I got work as a waiter so I could fund my own habit and by fifteen I was working more hours than I was in school. I was smoking a lot of heroin and I began to lose control.

"Then, just before I turned sixteen, my mother quit for good. She'd met an American guy – wanted to get married and get a green card, and having a kid with a police record wasn't going to help. I wasn't there when she went. There was no love lost. So she left and I was running around loose. The teachers wanted to wash their hands of me. I was expelled maybe twelve times from the same school and then they kicked me out for good. It just went downhill from there.

"But I guess, deep down, I had an instinct that I wanted to save myself. As I really hit the bottom, I decided I had to sort my life out. I went to my father's boss and asked him for a job. He sent me to Swaziland and Mozambique, gave me a lot of responsibility and it went very well for me. Fantastically well. I was out of drugs. I was working hard all day, physically hard. I was learning a lot and I felt like I was finding a place for myself.

"And then my mum found out where I was and put pressure on my father and his boss to get me back to Johannesburg and into school. The boss fired me and I ended up straight back in with the drugs and crime. I got into fraud, then robbery, and then I got a gun. I started seeing Gaylen but she made me feel vulnerable, so I broke it off. I formed my own little group doing hold ups, stealing cars to order, doing two or three video stores a night.

"A big part of me wanted to give it up, move to Mozambique and live in the wild up there. But of course there's always a final job and for me it was a house robbery with one of my drug buddies. The victim was an Irish guy, very strong, and there was a fight. The gun went off and bullets hit the wall either side of the guy's head. We were arrested at the scene. It took three months to come to trial and I just felt very tired."

In the end, William received a twenty four year sentence. It was the tenth of July 2000 and he was seventeen years old.

"You need to figure out how to stay alive in there," said his father, ever practical, as he said goodbye to him after the trial.

"I walked into prison and I thought: nobody's going to tell me what to do or give me any shit! I was probably frightened, so I over-reacted. We were locked in a cell twenty four hours a day, a tiny cell with a hundred and thirty people sleeping in shifts. We saw sunlight maybe once a week. I joined a gang – the twenty-sixers – which supplied drugs. Everything has a market in prison, food, servants, sex, drugs, and you need money to have a life. It was very violent with people getting knifed and killed.

"Five months in, I was transferred to the juvenile wing in Sun City and as soon as I got there, there was this sense of possibility. There was a lot more space and we weren't locked in a cage. I had one or two options. I arrived on the fifth of December and on the night of the sixth I made a decision. For me it was a watershed moment. I decided no more drugs, no more screwing around, no more whining. I realised there was nothing rebellious about what I was doing. If I really wanted to rebel I'd actually have to do the exact opposite, difficult as that might be.

"It was easy to stop the drugs, but quitting the gangs was much harder. They hate deserters and I ended up in solitary for my own protection. Then I met Lesley Ann and it was a turning point. It was like she was a beacon of inspiration, almost too good to be true. I struggled to believe she wouldn't lose interest in me. She was there to set up a programme in the prison and after two or three meetings she asked if I would work with her.

"I got busy, began to write a journal, wrote a hundred and forty eight pages on what I was ashamed of, and still I hadn't finished. I started to think about what makes us human and how we're all connected. I thought about it like I was a spider in the middle of a web, joined up to all the people in my life as well as lots of people I'd never even met, and with every one of them I seemed to be a negative force. Facing up to that was very hard. I thought about finding myself and then I thought: does anyone ever really do that? I decided it was more a case of working out who I wanted to be and becoming that person.

"So I started to work with Lesley Ann and Khulisa. I got together with a group of inmates, eighteen of us, and we began running programmes for kids who'd come and visit from the outside. We'd talk to them about crime and its consequences and why they shouldn't waste their lives. We started peer drug and HIV counselling. AIDS was huge in the prison, with people dying every week.

"We formed this incredible brotherhood, working together to do the best we could. Some of it was very chaotic, very hit and miss, but a lot of it went well. Being the leader of that group is probably the thing I'm most proud of in my life. I felt like I could dream something and then make it happen.

"At the same time I was doing all this informal work for the authorities. I had a laptop in my cell and I earned money by writing CVs for disillusioned prison officers who wanted out and needed to find a new job. I was writing performance reviews for staff – hundreds of them. It saved the bosses a lot of work they didn't want to do themselves and I guess it bought me favours. Then, towards the end of my time, there was a special police raid, cell by cell. They went crazy when they found copies of the security procedures and staffing rotas in my cell. They thought I must have stolen them, broken into who knew how many offices and filing cabinets to get them.

"I said, 'You don't get it, do you? I write them.'

"They were really embarrassed as it was meant to be a model prison, so the whole thing was just hushed up."

~

Later, as the sun went down on Blouwberg beach, we talked about shame and remorse. Forgiving himself didn't seem to be on the cards for William. I thought about what had really brought me back to see him, just as I had gone back to see Abdullah. He had promise, yes, but then so did many other people. It was his spirit that felt familiar, despite the gulf between us in life journeys. I sensed his pain, passed unwittingly from one generation to the next, pain that I often recognised in the people I came across through Quests, the damage sometimes done in early childhood and the huge and concentrated effort required to break the cycle. The gap between victim and perpetrator, between oppressor and oppressed, seemed tiny to me in that moment. A person could apparently move from one role to the other very easily, barely noticing what was happening to them.

I'd come to see William because he had taken a broken life and was turning it around. In a world with too few stories of redemption, he was rediscovering dignity, having almost lost it, and taking responsibility for who he was. And if William could do it, I thought, so could other people.

"You can't atone for water that's passed under the bridge," he said. "I've come to think that life's about what you do every day in every kind of way. I've screwed so many people over in my life and I can't afford to do any more of it now."

The spider's web of my own imagination was made of dreams and possibilities and the generative impact of one good deed upon another. William's web, so far at least, had largely fed on anger and an acute sense of his own role in things. His greatest fear, I think, was that of his own potential, if he stepped into the light and saw himself there. His greatest challenge was to learn to love the person he was and to know he was worthwhile.

We spoke about the future and what each of us had to learn and do. William wanted to change things on a grand scale – though he hadn't really worked out what that meant – and to make some kind of contribution to the world. It seemed to be difficult for him to settle for the ordinary, rather than retreat into solitude – to find the courage to stay in the moment, even when it appeared mundane. Yet I sensed he needed to do more of this. At the same time, I saw him as a teacher. He had a story to tell.

"I want to ask you something William," I said as we walked back to the house from the beach. "We're doing a lot of work in Africa right now. We have a big Quest coming up in South Africa, and then another one in Kenya. Why don't you come and work with us? I can see a lot of possibilities for you and I think you have something to give."

He accepted, and a short while later William moved up to Nairobi to base himself there, as we set to work preparing a particularly challenging Kenya programme.

Chapter Eight
What Role for Business?

In parallel with our learning about the capacity for hope and change in individuals like William, I also believed that Leaders' Quest had a part to play in the growing debate about the role of business in the world. Our Quest with the investment managers in Nigeria had been one small example of it. The debate over ethics, fairness and the way resources are shared was becoming more urgent, accelerated by the 2008 financial crisis. Regulation appeared unable to keep pace with the organisations it was designed to govern. Enterprising people often resented the blunt – usually belated – intervention of governments trying to change the rules of play, yet appeared unwilling to take the lead in modifying their own behaviour in the wider interests of society. These were difficult issues to address, but choosing to ignore them looked like an unsustainable response. Business leaders were being asked to acknowledge hard questions about their role in shaping the future, even though they knew that, sometimes, they lacked adequate answers.

As we explored these issues, one of those who emerged as both teacher and fellow traveller, was Professor Subi Rangan from the business school INSEAD. He and I first met in 2004 when Subi joined a Quest in his home country, India, and the foundation was set for an inspirational working partnership.

"It was like having a lot of apples drop on my head – moments of profound realisation," Subi said of the Quest, later.

Formally a teacher of strategy and management, Subi is, in practice, a professor of life with a deep interest in most subjects, but especially philosophy, economics and science, and the seams between them. He and I struck up a sporadic dialogue about designing a Quest together one day. We discovered that we shared much common ground, but had arrived where we now stood via very different paths. Subi was a political scientist-turned business strategist who was increasingly curious about – and concerned by – the way in which he saw capitalism evolving. He believed in intellectual rigour and insisted on proving every argument, trivial or large, with systematic logic. I, on the other hand, tended to work intuitively, frequently trusting my instincts well before I could actually prove whether something was true or not. But we respected one another, appreciated our differences, and so decided to find a way to collaborate. The result, in February 2008, was a joint eight-day leadership programme between INSEAD and Leaders' Quest, designed for senior leaders from multinational firms. We called it AviraQuest – which stood for awareness, vision, inspiration, responsibility and action.

Embedded in AviraQuest was an idea for which Subi coined the phrase, "Business 3.0". It included asking how people's expectations of business were changing and how capitalism needed to evolve to be fit for the future. We began to pose the question: if we are currently living with version "2.0" (or in some cases even "1.0") then what does a "3.0" iteration of business need to look like? And what has to change to deliver such a shift?

Helped by Subi's insight, our Quests began to encourage leaders to ask tough questions about themselves and their own purpose, and then to craft smart and creative responses that could be rolled out in their organisations when they returned home. This meant looking imaginatively at the core competencies of a business, and finding ways to go beyond the obvious.

Change is rarely the result of a single factor. The inspiration for new thinking almost always comes from multiple sources. But, over time, we came to believe that the experiences and reflection that a Quest provided could help spawn worthwhile innovations in NGOs, social enterprises and, perhaps most powerfully of all, given their span of influence, in companies too.

There were many examples. They included the head of a material sciences business who, following a Quest in India, looked at the products his company made and asked: "What else can we make, using the knowledge we already have, to improve people's lives in new and creative ways?" Three years on, the resulting innovations (all of them commercially viable) included low-cost building materials to construct replacement housing for slums, and affordable lightweight prosthetics for people who had lost limbs. Another example was the CEO of a global software firm who used the Quest as a catalyst to rethink his company's contribution to sustainable living. He challenged his team to redouble its efforts to design software which measured the environmental impact of business activity – carbon footprint, transport costs, air and water pollution. It was already providing thousands of customers with the tools for measuring the financial performance of their companies. Why not environmental performance too?

"We worked out that our customers produce one sixth of the world's carbon footprint," he told us. "Helping them to reduce that will make a far bigger contribution to the planet than anything we can do on our own."

These were the kinds of leaders we most wanted to work with. They were prepared to rethink what was possible, to find the resourcefulness to act, despite having no certainty of outcome. The challenges of shifting the present state were often extraordinarily daunting. It was one thing to start a business from scratch and embed in it the values you thought were most important, but to drive culture change in a big, long-established corporation was invariably hard and called for wisdom, courage and determination.

~

A couple of years on from the start of the 2008 financial crisis, I was invited to Canary Wharf, in the heart of London's financial district, to meet the CEO of one of the world's largest retail banks. He had joined a Quest a few months earlier and the experience had made an impression on him. Now, he was in the midst of navigating his company through the long-running global economic downturn which continued to unfold, impacting huge swathes of society. The banking sector was under fire from many quarters for the part it had played in precipitating the crisis. He'd invited me to come and share his thoughts about what it would take for his company to grasp how seriously the industry had fallen short of expectations. As I rode the elevator to the top of a huge and shiny glass tower, I found myself watching a strangely apt live news feed, playing out on the flat-screen TVs sited either side of the elevator door. It was the story of an effort to rescue twenty bank workers in Athens, who had become trapped on the top floor of a burning building after citizens protesting at their country's economic meltdown had set fire to the bank.

Our meeting, however, was a positive one. This particular CEO had a clear plan and had embarked on a bold journey to embed a philosophy of social accountability within the bank. It was an uphill task, in a sector that many people regarded as irresponsible and self-serving. Yet rather than be defensive, he'd chosen to look inside himself and the company and ask whether this bitter public verdict might be true after all.

We agreed to design a Quest for his top leadership team. It would take place in Kenya the following March. The goal would be to gain a better understanding of life on the ground in one of the bank's key markets, both for the minority of people in the country (and on the African continent) who could avail themselves of a bank account, and for the overwhelming majority who remained unbanked, and were often thought of as risky or unprofitable customers.

We set to work together to create what would be a complex programme, and our first ever Quest in Kenya. The Leaders' Quest team included people who had been with us from the earliest days, and others who had joined more recently, including William, who was helping us on a freelance basis. His role for this particular programme was to lead on logistics and, in particular, security, in a country where robbery and violence were sadly commonplace. Given William's background, he was better placed than any of us to assess the local risks.

When the time came, the Quest itself began with very sad news. The day before we were due to start, I awoke early to a text telling me that Naidu had passed away just an hour earlier. He was sixty years old.

I'd known he was fading for several months and had last seen him just five weeks earlier in Bangalore. I'd been there with a Quest group and, despite his failing health, Naidu had insisted on meeting us.

"I told my doctor I had to be well enough for this date. No matter what, I had to be here," he said.

We'd met with Naidu, along with two women from the fellowship programme, in one of their homes in the city's slums. The walls were painted pink and green and the small one-roomed house was surrounded by orange and yellow marigolds. We sat on the floor, drinking hot, sweet tea as we talked, with Naidu carefully translating each of their stories in turn. The first woman, Gowramma, came from a group of some four hundred migratory families who worked in the construction sector, moving from one building site to the next. Malnutrition and skin diseases were rife and they lived under plastic sheeting with no access to sanitation or clean drinking water. Over the previous year, as part of her fellowship and with the support of a mentor, Gowramma had helped many of the workers to unionise to strengthen their position with their employers, and to obtain identity cards. She'd organised a series of health camps which had treated over six hundred people, and had set up crèche facilities for some of the workers' children.

The second woman, Panchavana, had also entered the fellowship programme with great commitment. In the first training module, which focused on personal identity and purpose, she'd declared her desire to train as a mental health worker and work as a carer in the community. We had teamed her up with Naidu's organisation, BasicNeeds, so that she could learn the basics of mental health care. One year in, she had already helped several hundred people to access medical and financial support. Using the skills she had acquired through training modules on project planning and management, she'd also set up a day care facility for mentally ill people in Bangalore. Panchavana knew as well as anyone the effect mental illness could have upon families. When she was seven years old, her mother had abandoned her children while suffering from depression, and, after a year, Panchavana's distraught father had passed away, leaving her to take care of her younger siblings. Now, some twenty three years later, one of the people for whom she succeeded in finding medical care was her own mother, who had spent the intervening years living on the streets.

As the week in India had drawn to a close, we began to share our own questions. Each of the Quest participants was thinking hard about their own journey and what they would do differently when they returned home. One of them was a man who came from the Ukraine, where he was CEO of one of its largest companies. He was struggling to balance a life with too many demands, striving to do the right thing and live up to the challenge of leadership in a fast-changing nation. He was fearful of letting down his family, colleagues or both, whilst trying to find the joy in everyday moments. The simplicity of our fellowship meeting, the evident care and mutual respect in the room, and the openness of the discussion seemed to affect him deeply.

"When I get home, I'm going to go and visit the homes of some of the men who work in our mines and factories," he said. "I realise I have no idea of where or how they live. I want to go and meet them properly, to take my managers with me. I want to understand what life is like for them. It's strange to say that it's taken me being here, so far from home, to look back on my own country in a new light."

That visit in Bangalore was the last time I saw Naidu. As we left to walk through the neighbourhood, he stood, looking a little forlorn, and waving from the street. He was too weak to walk with us. Later, he sent me an email to say how much he'd enjoyed the day and how sad he'd felt at parting. "Mixed Feelings!" he wrote in the title line.

A month later, as I was getting ready to leave for Kenya, I got word that Naidu had been taken into hospital. In the back of a taxi on my way to Heathrow, I had my last conversation with him. He was in intensive care, speaking from his mobile phone and struggling to breathe, yet his customary dry humour remained.

"I'm in the hospital with an oxygen mask on my face," he said, his voice muffled and distorted. "Pleasure in pain…"

I sent him a farewell letter by email later that day, and his nephew Prajju read it out to him. Naidu was fully conscious, Prajju told me later, emotional and brave, slowly and deliberately despatching little last minute messages to and fro for the friends he was leaving behind.

Now, as news of Naidu's passing came, I was here in Kenya with colleagues who had also been close to him. We exchanged tearful hugs over a silent breakfast and then chose to delay the start of another hectic day, to sit together and reflect for a while on his life and what he'd left us with. I sat and laughed ruefully as I spoke about my own experiences of the previous twenty four hours, and how they would have amused Naidu.

I'd been to see the Nairobi centre of the Missionaries of Charity, to agree on final details for the forthcoming visit with a group of the bank executives that I was due to lead there in a couple of days' time. The centre had been established a few years previously in one of Nairobi's most notorious slums, by Mother Teresa and her Mission. Given the risk of violent crime in the city, the bank's protocol required us to make our Quest visits accompanied by plain-clothed security guards. We decided to spend time with them as part of our final preparations, so that they would understand the nature of our work, and the trusting relationships we had established with local communities.

So it was, that I found myself in the company of three Kenyan security guards whose job it was to assess the risks of our programme, as I set off to visit the nuns of the Missionaries of Charity.

Two of the men shared the name Fred, and the third was called Boniface. One Fred was at least six foot six inches tall, broad, and dressed conspicuously in a smart, shiny black suit with polished leather shoes and dark, wrap-around sunglasses. The other, like Boniface, stood around five foot six inches, in a skinny suit and matching shades. I chatted on the journey with the three of them, about their work and ours, and they became steadily more interested as the drive wore on. Eventually, we turned out of the dense, choking traffic of a pot-holed road, to cut down a dirt track that ran through a mêlée of huts and street vendors. We pulled up in front of a walled compound that housed the nuns and their work. A noisy gaggle of curious children emerged from the surrounding shacks as we climbed out of the car, and we had to step around several disabled women, huddled on the ground begging, in order to reach the compound gate. A gang of youths hovered, dressed in rags, several of them sniffing at glue bottles, as straggly goats, chickens and stray dogs foraged through piles of trash and rotting food on the ground.

Big Fred stood for a moment surveying the scene, and then he sucked in his breath and let out a long, low whistle through his teeth, shaking his head solemnly. "This is no good at all," he said. "I'm going to have to call for back up."

My heart sank. This was way past being funny. "You've got to be joking!" I exclaimed, confident he wasn't.

"Well frankly," Fred replied, "we could be attacked by a goat!" He began to relax and laughed out loud, safe in his assessment that our visit to this part of the city, despite its dubious image, would be a safe one.

I laughed then too. We all did. Apparently we were on the same side, and today, their security detail would be an easy one. "You're on a Quest!" I said. "Why not just enjoy it?"

They grew curious. None of them had any idea that Mother Teresa's Mission was here in Nairobi, tucked away in an area that was feared by reputation. Waiting for us inside the compound was Mary, the resident social worker who had planned the visit with me. With her was Sister Lizelle, who stood around five feet tall, a beautiful, round bundle, positively bubbling with joy. She'd spent ten years training with Mother Teresa before being sent from Calcutta to take up her post here. As we made our way round the facility, meeting different members of the community, she broke into a rolling laugh of pure happiness at regular intervals. She picked up babies, played with children, and wrapped her arms around the old women who shuffled up to greet her, eager for the warmth of human touch.

Fred, Fred and Boniface, along with our driver Joseph, looked stiff and awkward as if they rather wished they could melt into the ground. In the disabled children's room there was one young boy who couldn't walk. He'd learned instead to manoeuvre himself around very rapidly, by flipping his lower body, like a fish swimming across the floor. The boy took one look at all of us and, noisy with excitement, began to flip-flop his way over towards the larger Fred where, with great effort, he launched his torso against a pair of tree trunk legs. Then, to Fred's evident horror, the boy began to climb – somewhere between a jerking and a swimming motion – and to pull himself increasingly upright against Fred's rigid frame. Looking horribly conspicuous and with no way of escape, Fred took the boy's hands and nervously began to help him upwards. After a moment, very hesitantly, Fred's feet began to move – small steps, from one foot to the other, in a taut little dance that was the beginning of play. The child whooped with joy, totally unselfconscious. Sister Lizelle clapped her hands together in delight and pealed with laughter. Fred swayed to and fro, broke into a tentative rhythm, and then began to smile.

From here, we went to a room full of babies, all of them abandoned on doorsteps or left in dustbins, collected by the police and brought to the Mission. The men were all fathers themselves. We melted and began to coo and play and pull silly faces at the infants.

Our final stop was the place where the older ladies lived – typically women abandoned by their families because they'd become a liability through physical disability or, more often than not, dementia.

"Don't be frightened of them," said Sister Lizelle, very jolly now. "They may want to touch and hug you and it's just fine. They're only being friendly."

The men's faces settled into a kind of resigned dread. They trailed along behind me down the corridor, wearing rubber flip-flops on their socked feet. We'd all been asked to remove our shoes to keep the floors clean. We walked into a babble of voices, singing, clapping, the occasional shout and a reaching out of hands to touch us and stroke our arms and faces. Ladies, large and small, hair wild and neat, smiling and grimacing, shuffled up to greet us. There was nothing for it but to surrender – to join in and make a party, to dance, to sing and play like children. We were simply being welcomed.

When the time came to leave, I had to tear the men away. They were deep in conversation with Mary, full of questions. They wanted to know about adoption and the future prospects of the children we had met. Would these kids have families to raise them? Could ordinary people like them adopt a child into their own family, or did they have to be rich? What would it cost?

"You know," said big Fred turning to me as we left. "This is the best day's security work I've ever done!"

As for Naidu – well, he would have loved it all. He'd have found joy and meaning in every minute. And he'd have chuckled generously at the irony of me, and four grown men, wilting, softening and finally celebrating in the face of Sister Lizelle's irrepressible and infectious love.

~

The Quest itself was a great success. It felt like an example of collaboration at its best. Our team came together to lead thirteen different streams of visits, each for a group of around ten executives from the bank, and the surprise star of the day turned out to be William. At the last minute, one of our colleagues fell sick and I asked William to step in to support him. As luck would have it, the group turned out to include the bank's Chief Executive. William, however, was completely unfazed. He gathered everyone over breakfast, introduced himself, and then set out for Kibeira, one of Africa's largest slums, to spend the morning with a youth project working on ethnic co-operation, gender equality and economic empowerment. This was followed by lunch with an entrepreneur, recently returned from Silicon Valley, who'd established a scholarship programme for bright children from poor backgrounds, and was now advising the government on plans to develop a high-tech park to kick-start the country's focus on the knowledge economy. Finally, the group finished with a meeting with the CEO of Kenya's largest mobile phone operator. William, I heard later, had done a superb job, steering proceedings with poise, and taking care that everyone, hosts and participants alike, gained as much as they could from their meetings with each other.

I was reminded throughout the Quest that between all of us, there is only ever a degree or two of separation. As I ventured out again with the two Freds and Boniface, this time in the company of some of the bank's leadership team, I asked my three new Kenyan friends to help lead the visit. We went back to the Missionaries of Charity, to Sister Lizelle, Mary, the babies, the children and the older ladies. Our three protectors stepped out with pride, making introductions, enjoying the familiarity and building on the rapport they'd established just a few days earlier. And this time there was an added twist.

"I'd like you to meet with some of the street children who live around the Mission," Mary had said. "If I invite some of them here, will you meet with them? Just to talk? They'd really like to see you and they have so little in their lives."

"Of course," I said. "How many do you think will come?"

"Oh, just about twenty," she'd replied.

At least forty children showed up. It was hard to tell, but they looked between ten and eighteen years old. The food that Boniface and Joseph had brought to share with them, on behalf of all of us, and which had seemed like far too much as we set off for the day, now looked woefully inadequate. We distributed loaves of bread, packets of biscuits and fruit drinks. Immediately all conversation ceased as each and every child wolfed down the food in front of them in seconds, literally tearing open a loaf of bread and eating it whole in a few massive gulps. It was shocking and humiliating to behold such hunger. And then to sit and try to respond as they asked us how they could find work. The desperate need that I have seen so often echoed the world over – to get a job, to earn a living, to have a sense of purpose.

We took our leave reluctantly. Our plan was to drive an hour or so out of the city to visit a micro lending project which worked with farmers in the surrounding villages. Its goal was to help the farmers purchase livestock, typically funding a single cow or goat at a time, or to buy seed or basic farming equipment. We visited some of their homes, looked at the crops they grew, the livestock they raised, and spent time talking about their lives and what they dreamed of achieving for their children.

Later, as the sun dipped lower in the sky, we sat out under a tree with a gathering of some fifty farmers. The men sat on one side, the women on the other, many of them with small children in their laps. They had learned that their visitors were bankers and they had some questions they wanted to discuss.

"Some of us here have lost goats and cows, and some have lost their shacks in the past two years, when loans have been called in by banks and money lenders," said one. "Our lives got very tough when the financial crisis came in Europe and America, and suddenly, we too were hit. How could that be?"

This felt surreal. Here we were, in a village in Africa, responding to questions about the global financial crisis. I couldn't quite believe that a link between decisions taken in London, Frankfurt and New York could reverberate all the way out here. But one banker found his voice and started to explain that, yes, these things were all connected – the careless, unintended consequences of decisions made in one place or another, in an ever-shrinking world. Even this ignoble tale of interconnection, it seemed, was a real one. Who was really to blame I wondered? And didn't blame just deflect responsibility and avoid some of what was most important? I remembered a conversation with a German friend, a scientist by training, just a little while before.

"Lindsay I want to tell you something I don't dare tell my wife," he'd said. "I think mankind will lose the battle to build a sustainable world.

When you and I know as much as we do, and yet still we don't change our behaviour enough, then it's hard to have hope."

But now, here in Kenya, I didn't feel hopeless. Rather, I felt a growing sense of possibility. It had almost sneaked up on me and I could sense it best with my eyes closed. Month after month, I was out in the world, meeting all kinds of people, and I felt that more of us were beginning to confront the idea that some things really had to give. Recognition, sometimes reluctant, that personal behaviour, and the systems and rules by which we organised our lives, were badly out of balance. There was a realisation too, that many people, possibly most of us, had somehow misplaced our own responsibility for the whole. It was nothing I could prove. I simply felt a swell of optimism, as if touching a well-spring of shared consciousness, the energy and connection the human spirit craves. The visit to Kenya was just one small expression of it.

On the final morning, as we took stock of what everyone had learned, I was delighted by the depth of commitment generated amongst the company's leadership over the course of three days together. They were humbled and inspired by what was possible. They had new ideas on how to take their core skills and apply them more widely – to think, for example, about how to provide finance and expertise to micro lenders, who in turn could deliver affordable loans to those who really needed them. They wanted to offer basic finance education to some of the millions of people in all of their markets – those at risk of falling into debt, often through a lack of knowledge rather than a lack of income – on how to manage household spending and saving, and how to plan and borrow.

This was not about charity programmes or corporate social responsibility in the conventional sense, admirable though these might be. It was a shift in perspective that spanned the future and the present, the extended network – seen and unseen – in which they played a part, and the idea that everyone is a stakeholder. It was also about growing a culture of service and contribution that, crucially, required something of a leap of faith. It would be driven by an effort to do the right thing, despite a lack of quantifiable proof that this course of action would make the company more profitable or sustainable.

Perhaps most important was the growing sense, across the leadership team, that these new goals were about getting to base camp on the "responsible and sustainable company" mountain, rather than making an easy run to the summit. This level of change required a long-term undertaking. Success – and the will to stay the course – was far from assured.

Six months on, the bank's leadership came together again, this time in Europe. They invited me to join them, to comment on some of the work they'd done since the Quest. It was a conference in a big hotel and the last thing I expected to feel was uplifted. I listened to the difficult conversations that were starting to unfold – about capitalism and how it needed to adapt, about inequality and fairness and the role of the financial system in all of this. We talked about the new projects underway since Kenya, and I was excited by how much had been accomplished in such a short time. I felt I was looking at people who cared and who wanted to be proud of who they were and what they did. There was a deepening understanding that their role was far broader than they had imagined. There was energy to drive greater transparency in the business, and willingness, amongst this group of senior leaders, to roll their sleeves up and get involved. I came away inspired and hopeful for the actions they were taking, and the changes they were making. These were courageous, early steps in a marathon. It would be easy to be cynical, safest too, perhaps. It was not yet a done deal and no doubt many challenges lay ahead in a tough corporate environment. But it felt like a powerful beginning and I was happy to see it.

Chapter Nine
Showing Up

The summer of 2010 came around, and with it our annual Leaders' Quest retreat – four days away as a complete team, to take stock and plan for the future. We met in Sweden at the farmhouse home of Max Metcalfe, who'd recently joined us to lead our work in India. Prior to joining us, Max had spent a decade with the Swedish retail giant Ikea, helping to clean up supply chains across south Asia, supporting and sometimes coercing factory owners to cut waste, reduce pollution and address child labour and poor working conditions. His pattern was to spend most of the year working in Mumbai, and then take a month in the summer, to think and recuperate in splendid isolation at his farm on the southeast island of Öland, off the Swedish coast. In the middle of July, around twenty five of us pitched up there to invade the peace.

The week began with baking heat. I arrived a day early to help with a massive shopping exercise, to buy in provisions and prepare rooms in the neighbouring ostrich farm as there were too many of us to fit into Max's house. Hours before everyone was due to show up, he and I returned from a shopping trip to find a horrible stench had permeated every corner of the house and garden. The farmer whose land abutted

Max's house, had, it turned out, auspiciously chosen this as the day for his annual muck-spreading fest. That morning he'd loaded several tractor wagons with tons and tons of cow and pig manure and then dumped it across all of the surrounding fields. The impact was instant and distressing. Then, just a few hours later, the flies emerged. A staggering infestation as millions of them hatched in the warm, steamy dung and took flight for next door.

Max gamely set off back to town to buy armfuls of luminous green fly swats in time for everyone's arrival, and we all settled into the garden for the first couple of days, wielding our fly swats in the shade of big chestnut trees, and working in small groups with flip charts as we brought together our ideas about the direction of our work.

We had several persistent questions to address. They included deciding which countries to focus on, and how to continue to enhance the impact of Quests, on our participants, and those we visited. We wanted to strike a balance between working with companies, and ensuring we could fund scholarship places so that leaders from NGOs, academia and the arts could also take part. We were far more interested in changing the world than making money, yet, without income from people willing to pay for our services, we couldn't survive. Finding the sweet spot between impact and financial security was an enduring challenge.

Our own internal culture mattered too. We could hardly encourage other people to be open, transparent and generous if we weren't doing our best to model that kind of behaviour ourselves. This called for regular open discussions between members of our team and a willingness to grow as individuals. It meant finding ways to celebrate the best in everyone while also owning our own limitations and missteps. Spending time in this way was just as important as planning next year's finances or designing future programmes.

We worked late each day, mapping new ideas on big sheets of card which we stuck up on the walls, before barbecuing dinner together under huge, translucent northern skies. The sun stayed up till way past ten and rose again shortly after three. On the third day, the sky darkened and streaked with purple clouds and we moved indoors and lit a fire in the sitting room as a fierce rainstorm raged outside. The house grew increasingly muddy, with damp cut grass spread across the wooden floors in little trails, left there by a constant stream of comings and goings in rubber boots and flip-flops. And then the sun came back.

Towards the end of the week we sat together in the garden and talked about our own leadership and the responsibilities that came with it. I had led much of the proceedings so far and spent several days in preparation. I'd set out how I saw the opportunities before us and we'd debated a dizzying array of choices before narrowing them down to firm commitments for the coming year. I could feel a familiar tautness, the stretch of knowing I had lots to do in the months ahead, and could just about manage it. I felt the loneliness of being the person with whom the buck stopped. I had invested so much of myself in Leaders' Quest.

We decided to take a break, and I set off across the garden with Mark Norbury, one of our partners based in London. Tall and broad, Mark has the air of someone who can effortlessly carry half the world on his shoulders.

We sat down on the grass to talk and then lay back to look up at the sky. The ground felt firm and baked hard by weeks of sunshine, despite the recent rain. The meadow was freshly mowed and sloped away slightly towards a low stone wall in front of us. There was a line of lilac bushes to the left and a crooked patch of tangled wild flowers to the right that led into another small field. A peacock was standing on the wall, stock-still. I closed my eyes, shutting out the luminous pink and blue of the sky, and felt my body melt into the earth and my mind expand into the breeze. A deep appreciation washed over me, a sense of hanging somewhere in space. We lay on the grass and talked about the relentless energy that drove each of us. We spoke of the deep satisfaction we derived from our work, and of the sadness that occasionally washed through us.

It was a sadness I'd known from early childhood. I pictured it like a great universal pool, the grief of separation, and the polarisation of people past and present. It was wasted opportunity, lost potential, failed relationships, an accumulation of human suffering in everyday life that was both inevitable and unnecessary. It had to do with a way of seeing the world as upside down, with so many priorities seemingly back-to-front.

There was the CEO in Shanghai, for example, glued to his BlackBerry and disconnected from the world, with a degree of influence on the lives of those around him which warranted much more self-awareness than he possessed. Or the Director of an international NGO who was so convinced of her own righteousness that she'd aggressively alienated a whole group of potential supporters, dismissing their desire to help and their ability to even have an opinion, on the grounds that they were rich and therefore couldn't possibly understand.

On the final morning, I got up early and walked out into the garden. There was a beautiful, hidden spot behind the house and I went and sat in the grass to watch the fields and hedgerows come to life in the long slanting sunlight. I wanted to be alone for a while. I thought about how the sadness also stemmed from a wish to help make things better; that it was important to use these waves of grief as a source of energy, and grow beyond them. Right there in the moment, as our time in Sweden came to a close, I found I could bring the sadness into view after all and let it go.

I recognised that my own fragility held a gift. It was vulnerability, the capacity I used every day to encourage others to step beyond their comfort zone and experience the world as it is. Without vulnerability, I would be without compassion. This realisation was like walking through my own giant window and out into the light. I felt the old sadness dissipate. Something inside me had shifted. I also knew that what I was learning about myself would soon show up in Leaders' Quest. It would shape, in some way, the choices we made next, as we figured out how we could be useful. I would be more open about the things I thought mattered most, even in the face of fierce resistance. I would be more courageous in standing up and saying who I was. And as I did so, I hoped the people around me would be freer to do so too.

~

With so much going on in my working life, I was continually looking for ways to include my family in what I was doing. The phrase "work-life balance" had never seemed to fit. Instead, I tried as much as possible to integrate it all. The children were well-known around the office, sometimes dropping in on their way home from school to find a spare desk and do their homework, curious to know what everyone was up to. Colleagues from overseas would regularly stay with us at home, sharing stories with the boys over breakfast or dinner. My husband David too, had an intense travel schedule of his own, and the way we spent time as a family was an important topic of discussion amongst the five of us.

Occasionally, when the opportunity arose, I would bring one or other of the boys along on my travels and each time it proved to be a precious time together. Now, David and I wanted to do something that included everyone. We decided to spend Christmas and New Year in India, travelling as a family, accompanied by David's mother, Leah. The trip would be a chance to introduce our children to some of the people who made the country special for both of us.

So it was, as 2010 came to a close, that the six of us found ourselves in the narrow alleyways of Rafi Nagar, in the vast slum of Govandi, home to Mumbai's largest rubbish dump. Also with us for the day was Rahul Gaikwad, who had agreed to come along to translate between Marathi and English.

Govandi is extraordinarily bleak if you focus simply on the physical infrastructure and overlook the spirit of its people. The landscape is one of undulating hills, cloaked in smoky mist which rises thick and steamy in the sun. It is a big, soft, rolling place, of earthen brown, splashed with primal colour – trash as far as the eye can see, and here and there a thin dusting of grass pushing up towards the light. Rahul told us that the municipal government had a vision that one day all this would be a garden, but it took a fertile imagination to picture it.

Our taxi pulled up in an open space, with the trash hills to our left and the higgledy-piggledy homes of Rafi Nagar on our right, and we climbed out of the car. Leah looked anxious and grabbed hold of Louis' hand as he stared about him wide-eyed and wrinkled up his nose.

"It's very smelly" Louis said, a bit too loudly, then clapped his fingers over his mouth with a nervous giggle, for fear of being rude.

We were looking out over a sea of hunter-gatherers, some as young as nine or ten, sifting through the wet of animal and vegetable decay. Small, bare feet, thick-skinned and chapped, which navigated shards of broken glass, crushed plastic bottles and twisted scraps of metal buried in the mound. Every day, thousands of men, women and children, with sacks on their backs, came here to tramp from dawn to dusk across seething dunes of discarded life, to pick and sort amongst the waste and salvage what they could to sell. These were some of the people known as rag pickers.

Rafi Nagar itself is built on rubbish. The sides of many of the streets run with sewage, for lack of any sanitation. At the far edge, tumbledown shacks stand in ranks and look out across a wide creek where a thin, toxic stream runs, surrounded by a vast sea of muddy waste. A long string of precarious wooden walkways, built on stilts, emerges haphazardly from the bank to project out, high above the creek with a steep drop to the sludge below. At the end of each of these sits a toilet, each one a silent sentry post in no-man's land, cramped, lop-sided boxes made of wooden slats with a gap in the planks to let the waste fall through.

David asked Rahul about the monsoon.

"The water comes up very high, to the knees and sometimes to the waist, and runs through all the houses," he replied. "Kids swim here when the water rises and malaria and typhoid are a big problem."

Everywhere was a profusion of life – goats, chickens, stray dogs, the occasional pig and thousands of people. Vendors plying their wares, women cooking on small fires, children playing in the mud or standing in line to collect water in big plastic jerry cans. Their homes were built of brick and wood or improvised from plastic bin liners, flour sacks and corrugated iron.

We were there to visit Anwari Khan, a warrior queen of the Govandi dump. She was one of thousands of vital cogs in the wheel that kept a city of some twenty million turning, in spite of itself. Between us, Anwari and I had the beginnings of a friendship. A few months previously, we'd agreed I would return with my family to see her and her children. We would spend time together, exchange stories and learn a little about one another's lives. Anwari had graduated as a fellow a year or so back and quickly emerged as a star of the programme. She had a seemingly insatiable appetite to learn, and to put what she learned to practical use. She now worked here as a self-made leader, part of a thriving informal sector. She had become the chief organiser of a women's federation to tackle issues that ranged from domestic violence and access to clean water and sanitation, to combatting corruption amongst police and local officials. Most of the women who lived here worked as rag pickers or piece workers, stitching embroidery. In just three years the network of self-help groups that Anwari led had swollen, almost unbelievably, to around eight hundred women.

Rahul walked us through a series of narrow streets to the family home. Anwari was waiting excitedly for us at the entrance to her alleyway, a big smile on her face. She stood there proudly, dressed in an orange patterned sari with her hair sleek and black and tied behind her head. Her eyes were lined with dark kohl and she wore gold earrings and green and red bangles on both arms. Also there to meet us were two of her daughters, her baby grand-daughter, and a colleague from the women's federation, named Roshanjahan.

There was an exchange of greetings, hugs and handshakes and an effort to memorise new names as we were ushered into a bright, clean home. A narrow bed stood in the corner and Anwari invited Leah and David to sit, whilst the rest of us settled, tightly packed on mats on the floor. Her home felt very welcoming, though repair works were underway as part of the roof had recently fallen in. When they were finished, she'd have a two-storey wooden construction, more spacious than most, beside the creek.

We began to talk. Anwari wanted to tell her story and in fits and starts the threads of history began to emerge, in a very matter-of-fact way. She was born in the state of Uttar Pradesh and moved with her parents to Mumbai aged around twelve. She was engaged at ten, married at sixteen and then gave birth to eight children – five girls and three boys.

"I didn't learn to read or write – just a bit of Urdu from the Madrasa where my father sometimes sent me. But my children – they are all literate," she said.

Her marriage was tough and loveless. "He's very violent, my husband, a drunk and a gambler. He used to beat me all the time and kept me locked in the house. But slowly, slowly I found a way to change, to take my freedom and stand up to him. Still today, he comes and goes. He hasn't worked for many years. Mostly he's gone, which works well."

"And how is your relationship now?" I asked.

"I hate him," she replied.

The family moved to Rafi Nagar about eight years ago when they could no longer afford the rent in their previous slum. About a year later, Anwari became involved in the women's group. Her eldest daughter had recently been married to a cousin at her father's insistence. But the cousin turned out to share his uncle's temper. Anwari was looking for a way to fight back against the violence she saw all around her, and so she joined the group.

"Soon I was taking more and more of a leadership role. I picked up on the case of a three year old child who'd been raped. The police weren't interested and didn't want to take any action. So I took the child to hospital and got a report. I went daily to the police station until they agreed to take action and pursue the man who'd done it. He was arrested and tried and sent to prison for seven years."

Her work picked up as a community leader. In time she heard about the fellowships, put herself forward and won a place. Training and mentorship followed as part of a peer group and she learned many new skills, focusing, in particular, on violence against women.

"Hasn't it been difficult, this work? It sounds very hard," said Zac.

"In the beginning people did terrible things, cutting our electricity, throwing stones, calling me bad names. They threatened us and falsely accused my son of crimes. But today it's very different. I'm respected. Behaviour has changed. Many people have learned a lot."

The family were curious to know about our lives too.

"How do you find it when Lindsay travels so much and is so often outside the home?" Anwari asked David, shaking her head as she did so, a little smile on her face. "How do communications go on?"

"Well … life is complicated. There's a lot of movement in our house," David replied loyally.

The boys chimed in to tell her that they could all cook and wash their own clothes (something of an exaggeration I thought, but Zac was adamant). Everyone was astonished that boys could do these things. Soft drinks arrived – Coca-Cola and Fanta – and the daughters brewed sweet, thick cardamom tea and cooked up a little fruity porridge, chopping up plump orange raisins to stir into the mix. The children swapped stories about school, class sizes, subjects studied, sports played. The gap seemed rather wide.

"How much does school cost?" asked Joe.

"120 rupees [about £1.50] a month." one of them replied. Joe was astonished, trying to fathom the economics.

Roshanjahan laughed a lot through all of this. Her courage strengthened by the fun, she turned to Leah with a question.

"In India mothers-in-law and daughters-in-law don't get on at all well. It's very difficult. So this is what I want to know: how is it with you? How do you two get along?"

"We get along extremely well. No problem." Leah said emphatically.

"And what do you feel, being here? Seeing our home and how we live?" Anwari asked the boys.

"Well ... it's not what I expected," said Louis. "It's very happy."

"Tell us about your work. What kind of things do you do?" Leah asked.

"All kinds. Whatever's required," she replied. "About a week ago one women of twenty four years committed suicide by burning herself to death. She was suffering badly at the hands of her husband and she couldn't stand it anymore. As she died she told the police she'd done it to herself. So they called for me right away. I came to her home and it was terrible, terrible. I washed her body and made her ready for her funeral."

"Before I began this work, I thought of myself as a zero, a nothing," said Anwari. "Today I know I'm a leader. I believe in myself. I know that I'm capable. And I get great satisfaction when I'm able to solve a case, to improve a person's life."

Joe asked how she and others managed, given they couldn't read and write.

"I use my brain. I think!" she said laughing. "When I go to the police station or to some official meeting, everyone assumes I'm literate because I'm confident. I know so many laws, so many facts. The way you speak, the way you look and carry yourself – this is how people judge whether you're educated."

Later, Anwari walked us through the community to meet some of her neighbours. One of them was a woman named Nafisa Shaikh, the mother of three daughters. Leah asked her whether they went to school.

"They're all in school!" Nafisa said proudly. "My parents spent the little money they had on our marriages to pay for the weddings and the dowries and none of it on education. I've had to teach myself what I know. And now I want two things. I want big careers for my daughters and I want to see change in the community. I want us to deal with the sanitation. The first responsibility for this is the government's, but there are also local people. We too have to change our environment."

I turned to Anwari. "Education, sanitation – these are such big issues. And yet so many of our fellows choose to focus their work first and foremost on violence against women. Why is that?" I asked.

"Because everything comes back to this issue. Everything is connected to the way women are treated and their ability to speak out. Without that, nothing can be addressed – not education nor sanitation nor health nor water ..."

As we came to part, I noticed another woman dressed in red and gold. She was watching us intently and I went over to speak to her. Her name was Badrunnisa Khan and she too was one of the fellows. She worked on the problem of access to clean water, she told us, and had conducted a survey of over six hundred households to compile facts on the problem and what it would take to address it. She'd learned about many things through the training programme, in particular India's Right to Information Act (2005).

"I've learned to use the Act to ask for information from the local government, to demand it. And eventually, with much patience and a lot of effort from many of us, we're getting answers. Answers about water and what we are entitled to. We're getting information that we can use to demand change."

This was new work for Badrunnisa. "I didn't used to believe in myself. I simply stayed at home. But the group I am part of has grown and we are close to eight hundred women now. I'm a different person to the one I used to be."

"How do you get all this done? Do you read and write?" I asked.

"Our version of literacy is confidence," Bandrunnisa replied, looking me straight in the eye. "And knowledge and information are our power."

That evening we sat as a family over dinner and spoke about the day. The children were thoughtful and energised by what they'd seen and learned. I felt very close to them, and grateful for the passion and understanding of three teenage boys, when faced with such complexity and inequality up close.

Chapter Ten
Rahul's Painting

A few months on, and I was back in Mumbai to focus on the next phase of our work in India. I'd felt for a while that we were on the edge of something new and were still trying to figure it out. The time in Sweden had been a catalyst, and the ideas that were emerging seemed natural and obvious, like an extension of our roots. No blinding flash of light, just resonance and a sense that a fog had lifted.

On one hand, through Quests we were working with leaders who had access to money and power, often people who were well known in their respective fields. Like everyone, they faced constraints and limitations, but they were typically people with more control over their destiny than most, and plenty of opportunity to shape the world around them should they choose to do so.

On the other hand, through fellowships, we were working with people who were largely unseen by those in power. They might be well-known and respected in their village or township but they were usually living close to the breadline, engaged in a daily struggle to make a positive impact. They generally had as much talent, energy and promise as any other leader, but lacked the opportunity to fulfil this potential.

Working with people at both ends of this spectrum was important. But the real opportunity lay in what we could do between them. These different leaders needed to connect, engage and listen to one another. Above all, they needed to build mutual respect and trust. So often, whether between business and NGOs, people with different political perspectives, or in the Middle East, I'd witnessed one set of voices shouting down another, as if success for one section of society required defeat for the other. Against a backdrop where people rarely voluntarily surrendered advantage, it seemed that fairness, and the capacity to stretch beyond self-interest and take the long view, were qualities in short supply. The next stage of Leaders' Quest would have to address the courage needed to share power, rather than simply keep and use what each person had.

To this end, I knew we had to cross an invisible line of our own. Our team was a reflection of our diversity. It included people like me who had built successful careers in business, academia and other fields. It also required the hard work of a new generation of colleagues, making different choices, and willing to build a career in a social enterprise like ours, where the financial rewards were rather different to those found elsewhere. And it included people earning very modest incomes, leaders from slums, depressed inner cities and impoverished rural areas, many of whom had seen little or no benefit (and sometimes quite the opposite) from economic growth and increasing globalisation.

We needed to integrate the work of Quests and fellowships and focus on the overlap between the two. This called for even greater trust and it had to begin with us. We needed to acknowledge some of our own dilemmas, even when there were no apparent answers. Could we really be a cohesive team – a tiny microcosm of the world – in spite of these divides of life experience and circumstance? Leaders' Quest included people who'd built their sense of purpose and identity on a struggle against what they saw as injustice. Now we were asking them to take that same passion and invest it in building relationships and common ground with people they'd long since regarded as the opposition. And there were others like me, for whom the next stage of growth meant looking more deeply at the fairness of the system in which we'd thrived, and asking uncomfortable questions about what we might have to change or give up.

There was probably no better place to wrestle with these questions than India, a country that seemed to magnify the contradictions of the world. Our colleagues there included leaders like Max, Jayma Pau, Sujata and Mahendra Rokade, each of them responsible for different aspects of our work.

After three years in our London office, Jayma had recently relocated to Mumbai to build the team there and grow our Quests. Sujata was leading the national expansion of our fellowships, working with Mahendra, who had joined her as a boy some years back when he had dropped out of school.

Born and brought up in Mumbai, Mahendra was now on his way to completing a post-graduate distance learning course on social work. As a Dalit he had grown up acutely aware of his place at the bottom of the Indian caste system's social hierarchy, yet somehow, as a young man, he had managed to let go of much of his own anger and indignity and see himself as a role model for the next generation. Consequently, he'd grown into a formidable leader in his own right.

The last time Mahendra and I had seen each other had been the previous autumn, when he had taken time out from his work with us, to jointly lead a hunger strike in his slum community, which was threatened with demolition. The people there had endured years of uncertainty, stuck in a log-jam of bureaucracy and graft, waiting to hear the fate of the land on which they lived. The government appeared to have done a murky deal with developers, though the facts of the case were unclear.

In a city where corruption was rife, activism and free speech played a growing role as ordinary people increasingly fought for what they thought was fair. The hunger strike was another example of people resorting to defiant, desperate measures to bring something to a head. Seven days in, the strike was called off after the government acceded to the community's demands to see the development plans and to receive assurances that they would be rehoused before the demolition commenced.

Now, a few months later, we were embarking on a different kind of challenge. Fifteen of us, from across our organisation, were in Mumbai for a three-day workshop to figure out our future, tucked away in a nondescript hotel in the north of the city.

We came from different backgrounds, political perspectives and life experiences. Our time together was not about negotiating common goals, because we needed more than that. It was about acknowledging the asymmetry between those of us with plenty of material resources and those with very few, and the inequality of our respective struggles. We were there to find a way to work together that went beyond anything we had achieved so far.

~

To begin with, we simply took it in turns to speak, and listen to what mattered most to everyone. Mahendra wanted to understand what we would fight for and where we'd draw our lines in the sand. I, on the other hand, wanted to talk about unity and community and what we had in common.

"This is all very nice but it can sound too vague," Mahendra said. "It's easy to be apolitical if you already have power!"

He spoke about his youth and what had made him who he was.

"As a boy, I was full of anger. Meeting Sujata and joining CORO saved me. Without that I would have pursued violence. With her help I was able to take all that energy and turn it to entrepreneurship and activism, to fight peacefully for change. But still our work is often a struggle against injustice. I wonder whether you are really part of that struggle?"

It was a tough question, given all the effort of the preceding years. But I understood him. Sometimes the work we did left me feeling as if I was standing on a fragile bridge in a raging storm. I too could find myself caught up in anger at some injustice or other. Mahendra's question reflected layers of mistrust and a history of disappointment. He had not seen the gap narrowed for his people and, like Sujata, he defined himself as an activist (a "human dignity activist" as Naidu would have called him), and that in turn required an opponent with whom to struggle. I, however, didn't think that Leaders' Quest could be successful with any kind of overt political agenda and I said so. I was happy for us to support Mahendra's right to fight for what he believed in, but collectively we had to stand for tolerance, open minds and a willingness to meet and to engage, whoever we were.

126

As the day wore on, I felt a creeping fear that I'd somehow over-stepped the mark in bringing this group together and expecting something great to come of it. Maybe it was for good reason that people typically stuck with their peers whose lifestyles, viewpoints and circumstances were the same as theirs. Who was I to be mixing it up – stepping in and out of different worlds and encouraging others to do the same? Late in the afternoon, with a queasy thump, I suddenly understood just how much we were asking of one another. It boiled down to fear and loss.

"I feel as if I have fallen in love with a wonderful idea," said Vilas, head administrator for the fellowships. "But I'm afraid of what I'll say to my family and friends; that if I support the growth and learning of powerful people too, the kinds of people you bring with you, they'll feel I've deserted the poor."

Then Gitika spoke up. Recently hired to work on Quests, she was a top flight graduate from a wealthy, middle class Calcutta family. Already her time with us had exposed her to people and aspects of life she'd never previously thought much about.

"I'm afraid I won't be able to live up to the task. That I won't have the courage to see this through and will be alienated from my family and classmates, who won't understand the choices I've made."

We talked about the people we feared we'd already left behind. In my case, I sometimes thought my own parents looked at my life with a mixture of pride and hurt and a sense that they'd lost some part of their relationship with me, that I'd stepped into a world they didn't understand. My argument that I'd just enlarged my circle of friendships and commitments was built on shaky ground. I could talk about expanding what was possible rather than negotiating trade-offs in time and energy, but perhaps this was a convenient delusion.

Now, gathered with the whole team in a meeting room in Mumbai, I was shocked at the responsibility we had for one another – like children playing with fire. I felt as if we'd broken some of the conventional lines that kept society divided neatly into different camps. We'd stepped into some kind of limbo land, where we saw ourselves and our relationships with one another afresh. We were a team, despite our differences, and would have to navigate, however difficult that might be, to find ways to stay connected and not to abandon one another. I had triggered much of this, and had to live with the consequences. I wondered if it might all go wrong, with some people left disconnected from their roots, uncertain of the future, with their sense of identity all muddled up. But in the end no one turned back.

We drew pictures on flip charts, broke into small groups to brainstorm and then came back together again to share ideas. The detail was so much more important than I'd thought. There were so many nuances, sensitivities of inclusion and consultation, all of which required attention and called for patience. We spoke about the work that was best done apart, where involving people from very different backgrounds would be a hindrance rather than a help. We discussed collaboration and the things that mattered most to each of us.

Finally, I tried to sum up what I was thinking and where I thought we'd got to.

"We have a shared vision and that's very important," I said. "It's based on common humanity. It's not about politics. It's about love and compassion and how we're all connected. Within our team we each have different roles to play. Some of us are responsible for Quests and for helping influential leaders learn. Others are responsible for fellowships and creating opportunities for invisible leaders to emerge and grow. But we each have to play our roles in the context of the same shared vision. I think that if we can really appreciate our inter-dependence, then a different kind of co-operation becomes possible. I know it's asking a lot of each person here – to take a risk and trust. Sujata, Mahendra, Vilas, I am asking that you care as much about the growth and well-being of a powerful leader as you do about the least empowered, and I am asking that those of us who work on Quests do the same. There's a place for political struggle, a place for advocating for one thing and against another. But that is not what we're here for. This work needs to be about everyone."

There was a long and thoughtful silence and then Mahendra stood up and spoke to the whole room.

"I am with you," he said, looking at me. "I am on this journey with you. I'm part of a much bigger world than I imagined. I want to tell you what I'll say when I next go to the villages and slums and invite the people there to meet with you and the leaders you bring with you.

"I'll say you've come to meet them, to listen to them, so that you can learn. I'll say you've come because you want to understand our lives – that you're here with mutual respect. I'll say to them: 'Yes! These people can support us and help us build our capacity to struggle for our rights and grow our skills! But they too have their struggles. Their lives are not all easy, though they may appear so.' I'll say we're here together so that each one may share his context, exchange thoughts and emotions. I'll tell my people that we too need to break our mindsets, to see one another differently."

It had taken us two days together to get there. Mahendra had led our breakthrough and we all knew it. We were ready to get on with the next stage of our work.

~

Three months after the workshop, I returned to India to help lead a Quest for people from the US, Europe and China. They were leaders from finance, law and business, social entrepreneurs and a couple of people from major NGOs. Rahul Gaware, one of our graduate fellows who now worked with Mahendra, had also been invited to join the Quest, as a participant in his home country. He too had grown up poor in Mumbai, in a family with very little formal education. At eleven years old, he'd begun to find his feet, volunteering with a mobile library which toured the local slums. Now he was studying in his free time for a law degree, yet he'd remained true to his roots, living with his wife and children in the slum where he'd grown up, and pursuing his passion for community work. On the first night, Rahul came to speak to me in the lobby of our smart hotel.

"Place feels uncomfortable," he said simply.

He wanted to stay at home, he told me, and come to meet us each day, rather than endure the dislocation of staying in a hotel in his own city which felt so alien.

"If you can stay Rahul, it will be a real gift for the rest of the group," I said. "Everyone's got so much to learn from you. And when we go and stay in the village in a couple of days, they'll feel as unfamiliar as you do now ..."

Rahul remained, weathering his own internal storm, and two days later a group of us travelled out of town to a small cluster of tribal villages where three of our fellows lived, deep in the countryside of Maharashtra. We were there to spend time with the villagers and to learn about the projects our fellows were working on to bring greater security to their own people. The villagers were mostly landless, dependent for work on the erratic needs of local farmers in order to earn any kind of living. In a country where caste still dominated many social interactions, these tribal people were widely seen as being at the bottom of the pile.

We spent the afternoon sitting under a shady tree in the searing heat of mid-summer, sharing our respective stories. The village men sat to one side and spoke first, reading from a carefully prepared speech and then replying to our questions, sometimes with laughter, yet always dignified, careful to explain lest anything be missed. After a while the women joined in.

"What are the differences in role between the women and men, in the work you do and how you spend your day?" one of the visitors asked.

A middle-aged woman stood up, pushed forward by her peers. "I get up at dawn and go to collect water for the family. The walk has got longer since the old well dried up," she said.

She was wiry and thin with a gaunt face and high, leathered cheekbones. Her feet were bare, her legs bowed and she wore her sari pulled up between them and tucked in at the waist.

"Then I make a fire and cook for the family before leaving for the fields. I work until the middle of the afternoon and then I come home to cook the evening meal. We eat rice and sometimes there are vegetables and then we sleep. There's no time for any more."

The men raised their hands, vying to speak first, before settling by some unseen consensus on a spokesperson, urging him to his feet. The man rose solemnly to address us all.

"I get up when it's still dark, well before four in the morning," he said. "I walk for two hours to the fields and I work without pausing till nightfall. Then I walk home. I eat no breakfast, only dinner."

The village men clapped in loud approval and the women giggled into their cupped hands, a few of them shaking their heads and rolling their eyes as they did so. The contest played on, between the sweat of one gender and the other, and the toil and tasks accumulated by each, over many generations.

Later, we played cricket with a bat and ball that someone had brought from England as a gift. The home team took a comfortable lead until fading light halted play, and the entire village began to converge on a central patch of ground that served as their regular communal meeting place. A meal had been prepared in our honour by a dozen or so of the women and everyone was invited. There was rice and yellow dahl, chopped okra with tomatoes and chili, and spicy root vegetables, all cooked in big, shiny metal pots.

A cultural evening, long in the planning, was to follow and a PA system, usually reserved for weddings, had been hired for the occasion. There was much excited to-ing and fro-ing and excessive rounds of "testing, testing", before finally, it crackled loudly into life and several elderly men stepped out onto a makeshift stage to play for us. They carried with them traditional instruments, the names of which were long and complicated, and settled on a row of plastic chairs that had been placed upon the stage. There was a pause as they took in the audience seated on the ground in front of them, and looked from one to the other, waiting for a cue. Then, with much ceremony, the little band struck up and began to make an awful din.

Soon – too soon it seemed to me – the women began to laugh, softly at first, holding their saris to their faces and then more and more raucously, hugging their sides as they did so and wiping tears from their cheeks, until the children too joined them, followed by the rest of us, unable to hold it all in.

The band members started to argue between stunted bursts of noise. Frustrated at their own disharmony, they slapped one another on the arms with each discordant note. One elderly gentleman, dressed in a white dhoti and matching skull cap, kept pouring water from a plastic bottle into the open end of a trumpet-like instrument, then shaking it, in an apparent effort to improve the sound. But it only seemed to make it worse. Eventually, the older women, undeterred by the piercing squeal and occasional boom boom from the speakers, took to their feet and began to dance, stomping, swaying and waving their arms aloft in the night sky. They pulled us to our feet to join them and we danced and sang and laughed together, mimicking one another's moves and hollering to the heavens. Li Qiang, a lawyer from Shanghai took to the microphone to sing a love song in Chinese, which went down far better than a clumsy rendition of "Stand by Me" by a handful of Britons.

And then, as even the hardiest began to fade, the village headman made a speech and presented us with gifts, before Mahendra stepped up to close the evening.

"These people have come to visit us," he said to the villagers. "They will sleep with us in our homes tonight and we are honoured to have them with us as our guests. They come because we are all connected, all part of the same world. They are not foreigners. They are human beings."

The village broke into loud applause and we made our thanks. We were to stay in the huts of local families who'd agreed to host us. I spent the night wide awake on an immaculately swept cow-dung floor. With me was a London-based asset manager named Anne, three local women and assorted children, all of us sprawled, uncovered in the sweltering heat.

At about two thirty in the morning, as everyone else slept soundlessly, a red-plumed rooster strutted several steps through the open doorway, his neck jutting back and forth. He stood, looking round him and shifting from one foot to the other. For a moment I imagined he looked me right in the eye. And then he threw his head back and let out a deafening cock-a doodle-dooo! No one stirred except for Anne, who was instantly awake, her eyes like bright marbles in the dark. For the next three hours we lay together rigid on the floor, contemplating a long day ahead and drifting in and out of crazy, wakeful dreams as the cockerel marched in and out every few minutes, crowing proudly.

At the end of the week, Rahul presented me with a painting he'd made after our return from the village. It showed a stick figure – him – standing outside a house and looking in at an open window. The scene inside was comprised of two distinct halves. To the right was all inky black and murky brown with nothing visible beyond the dark. And to the left, still indistinct, was the beginning of colour, a cloud lifting and the touch of something bright, swathed in muddy red and orange and the palest hint of blue.

"This is me looking in at my life after this week with you all," he said. "The darkness is how I used to see it – all bleak for my people. The colour is a new perspective, promise for the future, looking at my life through your eyes. It's the first time I've stood outside and looked in. I can't go back to who I was before. I'm changed. I see the world differently now. I don't know how it will turn out, but there is no going back to where I began."

~

Our work with communities like Mahendra and Rahul's continued to expand, and so too did our network of relationships with social entrepreneurs. They included people who'd created hybrid business models to combine profit with social purpose in ways that broke new ground. Increasingly we understood that one of the most useful things we could do was to share the stories of some of these individuals, and to serve as a community through which they could meet one another. Effectively what we were creating was a global network of people who shared an interest in improving the world around them, though often stemming from different points of view.

One such person who has been a consistent source of inspiration to Leaders' Quest over the years, is Garth Japhet from South Africa. Garth and I first met when he was CEO of Soul City, the social enterprise he founded in 1992. What began as a TV soap opera series set in a health clinic in Alexandra township, went on to become something of a legend on the African continent. A TV drama about the ordinary business of birth, life and death and the twists and turns along the way, the show was to become a medium for airing serious, everyday issues through the lives of its characters. It grew to be an extraordinary platform for social change.

One episode tells the story of neighbours emerging from their homes late at night, banging pots and pans in a wordless protest at yet another noisy beating inflicted upon a wife by her drunken husband. Roused from an uneasy, wilful ignorance of her plight, someone calls the police, as more and more people gather, clanging their saucepans together in a rising din, until the perpetrator emerges from his home, blinking and belligerent. He's arrested on the spot and bundled into a waiting police car. The day after the show was aired, a real life epidemic of pot-banging broke out, as people around the country spontaneously stood up to expose domestic violence in their own neighbourhoods. Incidents reported to the police rose by some seventy percent in the weeks that followed.

Soul City is about choices and how to make good ones. It hit a nerve and evolved into a hugely popular long-running series across eleven African countries, plus a radio show, mass media publications, and public health initiatives – all of them designed to use everyday characters to convey messages about values and the importance of making the right decisions.

In time, Garth was ready to move on. He left Soul City in the hands of the team he had nurtured, and set out on his next initiative. In many ways it was a natural progression. In 2010 he launched a new enterprise, Forgood, with the goal of bringing together and amplifying the efforts of multiple organisations and individuals, working across the country to transform the values of a nation. The idea was to mobilise people who wanted to be part of a nationwide movement for positive action. Adverts appeared on TV with well-known comedians performing unexpected acts of generosity: offering shoulder massages to people standing in the supermarket queue, serving sewage workers a surprise three course meal on linen-covered tables at the side of the road, or giving flowers to strangers as they passed them in the street. The concept was driven by the conviction that South Africa has somehow lost touch with the human values that make up a happy, healthy society.

"Noka e tlatswa ke dinokana," is the slogan. "A river swells from little streams." It includes media campaigns, outreach programmes and a social networking platform accessible online and from cell phones. Ultimately it's about personal responsibility – the notion that we need to move from "they should fix it" to "I can fix it".

"There are lots of people out there who want to do something good with their lives, but there are also others pulling hard in the opposite direction. All we're talking about here is something as simple as 'love your neighbour'", Garth told me. "I think of it as a law of being. We understand physical laws much better than metaphysical or spiritual ones. I know that if I run around naked in minus twenty degrees I'm going to die. But equally there's something that dies within me when I don't love my neighbour as I love myself."

As we sat talking, I noticed a photograph on his desk. It was a picture of Garth together with Anwari, the woman I had visited in Mumbai with my family the previous Christmas. Anwari and Garth had met there on an India Quest the previous year. He saw me looking at the photograph and his face lit up.

"I was so moved when I met her, so impressed," he said. "In spite of everything that's going on around her, Anwari's someone making great choices about how she lives her life. She could have followed many different paths, but instead, she's chosen to stand up and lead."

Later, I thought about the vision and impact of these two people and of so many more like them. It was as if some giant force was at play, connecting the energy of millions of people.

At Leaders' Quest we found too, that as our reputation grew, we would continue to be offered new opportunities to bring social entrepreneurs together to learn from one another. In May 2011, Zia Khan, Director of Strategy for the Rockefeller Foundation, joined us on a Quest and we started to explore ideas for collaboration. Ten months later we ran our first Quest in partnership, this time back in Kenya. We invited twenty of the world's leading social entrepreneurs to spend a week together meeting NGOs, businesses and innovators on the ground, to learn from practical examples and forge new collaborations with one another. It was a natural step, all part of an effort to help people move from hope and inspiration to concrete action and implementation.

Chapter Eleven
Shifting Ground

One year on from our meeting in Sweden, our team came together again for our annual retreat. The setting was an eco-farm in the county of Somerset in England. We were there to build on the work we'd begun in India with Sujata, Mahendra and others, and to share it with everyone else.

On the morning of the third day, a small group of advisors arrived to join us. They included the CEOs of two of our major clients, each of whom had agreed to come and talk about the impact of Leaders' Quest on their companies. There was warmth and humour as we went around the room introducing ourselves, with the occasional burst of Chinese, Hindi or Marathi and the quiet buzz of continuous translation in the background.

The circle reached Dr Mani, leader of one of the Indian NGO partners with whom we were working, in a bid to scale up the fellowship programme there. He was an activist through and through, having trained as a medical doctor and then spent much of his life working in marginalised communities.

"I think we need to speak about oppressive structures and inhuman capitalists!" I heard him interject with passion, part way through his introduction.

"Oh God," I thought. "Nice welcome!" I looked nervously in the direction of two of the very human capitalists who'd just arrived to give their time to help.

Mani was right, however. We did need to talk about what was fair and what was not. I found myself thinking about what had been most difficult in the preceding years. The effort to keep an open mind when wealthy people tell you they don't want to meet anyone who's poor, whether close to home or far away. It happens more often than you might imagine. The assumptions behind it are frustrating – that poverty equals misery, or that living in sometimes filthy conditions is a choice to which there are easy alternatives. That to be poor is to be ignorant and not to know what's in your own best interests. I still found it hard to take my disappointment at these reactions and turn them into possibilities, to stay generous, and remember we are all a product of our own histories.

In most of the situations I came across, power was fundamentally imbalanced and those of us with more of it were generally in no great hurry to give it up. But the asymmetry held its own pernicious bite. Fairness might be subjective, but extreme inequity was clearly not good for anyone. It ate away at the soul.

There were so many examples. I saw it in everyday situations between bosses and subordinates, departments and divisions. I saw it too in Israel and Palestine, though people on both sides would be furious with me for saying so. Many Israelis were held back by their own fear from giving something up in order to gain. For some of them there was also the belief that they might get away with refusing to participate in a process that would deliver a state to their neighbours. The Palestinians too, often seemed to be held hostage by their own extremists, full of rage and frustration at their predicament, sometimes fuelling the fear on the other side, and preserving the deadlock. It was fear of the "other"; the fear that one person's gain will be another person's loss and that the collective cake is finite.

We needed to talk about power, and voluntarily relinquishing it. About giving it up when you didn't have to do so. I was reminded of Adam Kahane's book, *Power and Love*,[3] in which he defines power as "the drive to self-realization" and love as "the drive to unity". We need both power and love, he argues, to break through our most entangled, sticky problems and create social change.

I knew what we needed to do, and I said so. We all had to shift, Mani included. He too needed to reach out to people whom he'd traditionally thought of as being on the other side – to step up with the courage he was asking of others. It was a two-way process and it was about the kind of trust that Mahendra had fostered back in India and then shared in the village. We needed to overcome that part of our own nature which depended for its identity on deeply held convictions, and to reach out to others with opposing beliefs, in order to go beyond, to a place of healing and progress. Because compassion, too, is part of what makes us human.

Next, it was the turn of the CEOs to speak, and the room fell silent. They told different stories about the impact of the Leaders' Quest community on them and their companies. They spoke about the new initiatives that had resulted. These included renewed focus on values and the way people treat one another in the workplace, innovative services to reach new markets, and cross-sector partnerships with NGOs. They spoke about the vision they had for their organisations, and their desire to combine commercial success with a positive contribution to society, even if the path to do so was still unproven.

"You've helped change the nature of the conversations we have," one of them concluded. "Today, when we're deciding whether to make an investment, the first item on the agenda is: what will be the social and environmental impact of this decision? It used to be at the bottom of the list, our last consideration. You've helped us shift our priorities."

This was more than I'd expected. I listened to some of our support staff, often somewhat removed from the sharp end of the work, as they began to ask questions, excited at what they were hearing. The stories the two CEOs told highlighted an important evolution in the nature of our work. We weren't just supporting them as they considered the context in which they operated globally. We were helping them to fundamentally change the way they thought about business, the way they made decisions, and how they chose to behave, on a daily basis, with their colleagues and their customers.

As I thought about the year ahead, I realised we needed to keep finding new ways for the leaders of some of the world's most powerful companies and institutions to co-operate with the leaders of the least powerful, stepping into one another's environments as they did so. We needed to focus on creating a sense of connection that would endure. The next wave of Quests, and whatever else was to come, would focus on transparency and sustainability and finding ways to share the best examples of these with an ever-wider network of people.

~

A few months after the retreat, we had an opportunity to put some of this into practice. We were contacted by the CEO of the technology company that was working to embed the measurement of environmental impact into its software products. He asked if we could develop a series of programmes for his senior leadership, to take place on different continents. The idea was to give their teams the opportunity to experience environmental and social challenges up close, and then to ask them to figure out how the business should respond. The first Quest would take place in Mumbai, with twenty of their leaders from India, including software developers, engineers and sales executives. It would run for four days, including two full days of field visits. The overall focus was to be leadership, sustainability and innovation. As it turned out, it would also include one of the priceless incidents that occur from time to time on Quests, to remind us not to take it all too seriously and to also have some fun.

The Mumbai programme got off to a great start and I woke on the third morning with high expectations. The day was to begin with a return to Govandi, Asia's second largest garbage dump, and home to a number of our fellows, including Anwari. After breakfast I set off by minibus, together with Gene, one of my long-standing partners, and ten of the Quest participants. Fifty minutes later, as I sat at the back of the bus, deep in conversation with the company's Sales Director, I was suddenly summoned to the front to speak with the driver. He was lost, he told me. A lot of translation and confusion ensued before he abruptly swerved to the side of the road and slammed on the brakes. Defiantly, he pulled out his instructions for the day, a stack of stapled papers, thrust them into my hands, then turned his back and folded his arms across his chest.

"Cosy Auto Tours", I read, and then "Urban Infrastructure Trade Delegation". There was a British government logo at the top of the page and a number of references to Norway that I couldn't understand. An awful realisation dawned. We were on the wrong bus. We had been brought to the wrong destination. We were not in fact the British (or even the Norwegian) Urban Infrastructure Trade Delegation. We were Leaders' Quest, and we wanted to go to the dump.

"Oh, no!" I cried. "This is bad. I need to speak to your manager – we have to phone him!"

Reluctantly, the driver pulled out his mobile, dialled his boss and handed me the phone. We spoke at, rather than with, each other, loudly and slowly, frustration rising. There was a minute of silence down the phone before a loud wailing began, "Oh my God! My God! Oh my Godfather, no!"

The British trade delegation had apparently arrived at the dump. They were hot and confused. They were in fact, at that exact moment, supposed to be at the Consulate for a high level briefing on infrastructure. Instead they were witnessing the lack of it, up close. They had climbed into our bus and ridden off at eight o'clock in the morning, and we had done the same thing, fifteen minutes later. Two different transport companies were involved.

"It's obvious what we should do," I said to the owner of the trade delegation bus. "We should keep your bus and you should keep ours! Nothing else makes sense."

The responses were many and varied, but all along the lines of: "Not possible madam, not possible…" and more wailing as the boss's colleagues in the office joined in. Then: "You have to get out of the bus right now madam. It has to go and collect our delegation immediately. Nothing else is possible."

"That seems like a very bad idea," I said. "We really need to swap buses."

The manager however, was insistent. My patience snapped and with it, all notion of altruism and standing in other people's shoes went right out of the window. I called our driver at the dump.

"Please empty the trade delegation off the bus now," I said.

By this time it was apparent to everyone travelling with us that a serious mix up had occurred. We clambered out of the bus and began to flag down a stream of auto rickshaws to take us to Govandi – more or less in the opposite direction to the one in which we'd come. Five minutes into the drive, wedged into a rickshaw beside the Sales Director of the software company, I began to laugh. He did too, and then we found we couldn't stop. The whole incident had felt like a nightmare right up to that point. Our schedule was packed and we had no room for a two hour detour before we'd even started. But the situation was simply too ironic, and suddenly nothing else mattered very much.

When we finally arrived, hot, dishevelled and disembarking in waves as the rickshaws found their way, our hosts were not in the least perturbed. Our excessive anxiety about time was not one they shared. An hour or so was neither here nor there. We would see what we needed to see, meet the people we needed to meet, understand the efforts they were making to generate more secure livelihoods for some of the fifteen thousand people who lived at the dump, working to recycle waste. Predictably, the visit was extraordinary and inspiring. I reflected afterwards that we should have simply invited the trade delegation to join us.

As the Quest came to a close, there were many outcomes to be celebrated. There was a renewed commitment to embed sustainability more deeply in the company's DNA; increased efforts to support rural projects in India and to figure out how to scale these; a pledge to provide funding for a computer lab, with a dedicated trainer to develop computer literacy skills amongst the women in one of the communities they'd visited; and a decision to provide some of the social entrepreneurs we'd met with the technological support they needed to tackle deep-seated social issues effectively.

But the most important development for me was a discussion with the CEO of the company's R&D facility, where four thousand people worked on next generation software.

"We were just so impressed by the time we spent with the fellows," he said. "The leadership these people demonstrate is awesome. I think we have a lot to learn from them."

We talked about possibilities.

"You know, there's something we've wanted to do for quite a while," I said. "Something we'd love to pilot with you. We'd like to design a joint leadership programme for your executives and our fellows. It would go far beyond a visit or exchange. So many of the skills and values we all need are just the same – vision, resilience, the capacity to plan and to make things happen. It would be a powerful message – people educated at some of the best universities in the world learning together with grassroots leaders who have dropped out of school. I think we'd find new possibilities emerging that neither peer group could ever imagine on their own."

It was an idea we'd first discussed a few months back with some of the fellows in Mumbai and the response had been heartening. They were excited to see themselves in this new light, as teachers as well as learners. I saw individuals stand a little taller, pride shining in their eyes. The software company's boss liked the idea too and we agreed to take it forward. It felt like an important milestone – the opportunity to put some of our most deeply held beliefs into practice, and the start of a new direction as we planned the year ahead.

Chapter Twelve
The Whole River

By the end of 2011, we'd completed a decade of work and I found myself wondering about the effort required to sustain whatever was to come. We had more than one hundred Quests behind us, almost eight hundred fellows in India and China, and partnerships with over one hundred community organisations. It had been a steep learning curve and I felt privileged and humbled by so much of what I'd experienced along the way. I was excited about the future, but at the same time I was also very tired. To continue running at the same pace looked like a daunting prospect, yet I was unsure how to slow down or look differently at the path ahead.

As I thought about all this, I decided there was still one person whom I wanted to see before the year was out and that was Yang Xin, the man whose photographs had made such an impression on me when we'd first met some eight years earlier. Yang Xin had hosted several Quests visits in the intervening years, sharing his story and talking about the huge environmental challenges facing China and the world. But this time I wanted to see him on my own, travelling with my friend and colleague, Jason, who'd offered to help with translation.

It would be a trip to complete a circle. Yang Xin's way of seeing the world had always seemed like a powerful metaphor for the work that we did in Leaders' Quest. He was one of the most inspiring, unassuming people I'd ever come across, though he would never have guessed it and it wouldn't have mattered to him if he had. There was also something personal about my connection with him. He was someone whose spirit spoke to me. The things he knew about life were things that I too knew deep down, had always known, though sometimes I struggled to say so. While I knew only a small part of who Yang Xin was, I sensed that his story, perhaps more than any other, would speak to my own. With Jason's help, I made contact with him in the autumn, and we arranged to meet a few weeks later in the mountains.

Jason and I arrived in the city of Golmud on the Qinghai-Tibetan Plateau in the early afternoon. It had taken us two flights and most of the day to get there from Beijing. In Xian, we'd almost missed our connection, lost in conversation whilst eating noodle soup. Now, in the taxi into town, we learned that Yang Xin's train would not get in until ten thirty that night. I'd been on the road for over two weeks and was due to leave for home the following morning.

"Never mind," said Yang Xin to Jason over a patchy mobile phone line. "We'll talk through the night."

He walked into Jason's room just before eleven pm, looking rather dusty, and dressed in a sweatshirt and jeans, with a small backpack over his shoulder and dried mud on his boots. The last time I'd seen him, his beard had been black. Now it was salt and pepper. His cheekbones were even more burned and polished than I remembered, and the lines on his face finely carved, as if sculpted by the wind.

"Will you show us where you've come from?" I asked, clicking onto Google Earth on Jason's laptop.

Yang Xin sat at the desk and a few seconds later we were looking at his camp, a five hour train ride away in the mountains. He and his colleagues were in the midst of building a second environmental station there, as a port of call for the nomadic herdsmen who passed through the area each year in search of new pastures.

I didn't need to tell Yang Xin why I was there. He knew already. I'd come to Golmud to respond to a spark of recognition from our first meeting. Since then, we had met only intermittently, when he came down from the mountains and our paths crossed in Sichuan, but I'd followed what he was up to on the internet and through his photographs. Now he was here to take us back to the beginning and tell us his story.

~

"I was born in Chengdu and lived there until I was seven years old," Yang Xin began. "But my memories of it are scant. It was only after we moved to Panzihua that I start to have memories. It was a small industrial town then, and my father worked in one of the factories there. But it was the surrounding nature that caught me. It's a beautiful, mountainous place and the river flows right through it. So I grew up beside the Yangtze in the high ground of Sichuan. And every hour that I could find, I played outside. You play differently in the country than you do in the city. You learn to catch birds, to fish, to fend for yourself.

"Mountains teach you a kind of initiative. The river was wide, hundreds of metres across, and we did many dangerous things. We were left to be free, to make our own judgments and to learn from our mistakes. Every year, several children would drown in the river. Children's curiosity is the most dangerous thing. But these were very happy years for me. I was friends with everyone – friends with the whole town. Each day we would get up early to play outside before school and then we would have just two or three hours of lessons. There was no pressure to study because it was the time of the Cultural Revolution. And after lunch we'd play again in the forests and the fields until nightfall.

"I learned that I had a relationship with the mountains and everything that lives there. I used to sit for hours beside the river and watch it flow. I saw that it was always changing, always moving, and it seemed to me that it continued on forever. And I thought to myself: I wonder where the river comes from?

"Then, when I was ten years old, I saw a map for the first time. It was such a special day! My mother brought it home, a gigantic map of China, and I was riveted. What caught my attention most was a thin blue line that started in Shanghai. I traced the line with my finger, traced it back across the country and, as it went I read the names of all the places it passed through until I came to our home place of Panzihua. I was very excited and I thought to myself: now I will know the answer to my question! Now I will know where the river comes from!

"So I followed the thin blue line with my finger, past Panzihua, back and back across the map until the names ran out. And still I had no answer. 'I can trace the river right across China,' I said to my father. 'But still I don't know where it comes from!'

"'I don't have the answer to your question,' he replied.

"I went to my teachers and I asked them too and each one gave the same reply. All except for one who said to me, 'I too do not know where the river comes from, Yang Xin. But why don't you go and find out?'

"I decided then that this is what I would do. And I kept it as a secret, buried deep in my heart."

His hands were small and swift and moved incessantly as he spoke, as if stroking a cat.

"I learned a lot from my father. He was one of life's great artists. He wrote poems and novels, he acted and he loved to fish. The crucial thing, with both my parents, is that they took my aspirations seriously, supported me in whatever I wanted to do as long as it wasn't bad. When I was sixteen years old and my parents sold their house, they used part of the money they got for it to buy me a camera. And that was the start of something special. I took pictures of everything in front of me! I was obsessed with what I saw through the lens – with capturing it. I even made a darkroom in the bathroom. But it was only later that I truly began to learn how to speak with the camera. At the age of eighteen I went out on my own, to Lijiang in Yunnan province, to Luguo Lake and Tiger Leaping Gorge. That's when I really started to take photographs.

"When I left school, I was sent to an accounting college and then to a job in a power plant, to work as an accountant. There was no choice in those days. You didn't choose your career. The government told you what to do and assigned you to a work unit. So that was my destiny. But still, I travelled at every opportunity, taking pictures, exploring.

"And then in 1978 the source of the Yangtze was officially named, and seven years later an opportunity came my way. There was a policy in my work unit, whereby you could leave for two years and try your hand at something else. If it didn't work out, you could go back at the end of it. So I left and went to Shenzhen on the coast to 'jump into the wild sea' as we used to say, and start a business.

"I hated it. It didn't work. And so I stopped and thought and then I came to a decision. I decided to go and find the source of the Yangtze. I planned a great expedition, the one I'd always dreamed of, and a year later a group of us travelled to the source of the river to navigate from there by raft, all the way to the sea. I was the expedition leader and the photographer."

"Tell me about the people who died," I said, remembering an earlier conversation about the ten explorers who perished along the way. "Were they all lost at once?"

"No, they died one by one – in rock falls, avalanches, ice floes. We knew when we began that not all of us would make it. We understood how dangerous it was. These were patriotic times. It was important that the first people to make this expedition should be Chinese. But I learned the two most important lessons of my life on that journey. I learned to see the whole river. And I learned that you never give up. Because of the people who lost their lives, the sacrifice that went into it, I learned that you never cast off any burden lightly. I feel a great responsibility for what they gave. It motivates my work. They died so that we could tell the story of the river."

"So what's happening to the river now?" I asked. "What's happening to the glaciers?"

"Here on the plateau, most of the glaciers are receding at a terrifying rate," Yang Xin replied. "The altitude magnifies the temperature change. We're the only people doing any kind of research on the Jianggudiru glacier, the source of the Yangtze. It's very difficult to get to. We presented a report last year at the World Economic Development meeting in Tianjin. It showed that in forty years the glacier had receded by more than four kilometres. People were astonished. They hadn't understood how fast it's happening."

"And what does it mean for the world?" I asked.

"It means that a population three times the size of Europe will become ecological refugees. That's everyone who lives at low levels in the Indian Ocean basin."

"Don't you get angry?" I said.

Yang Xin was quiet for a while.

"Think about it," he said. "Look at the area that will be affected. These are people who've contributed almost nothing to global warming. Many of them are incredibly poor and left behind. These are the people who will pay the price for our developed world, for the cities of Europe, America, India and China."

"And what will happen to the people of the mountains?" I asked.

"Everything will change for them. For people in high altitudes the glaciers are the source of life. They feed the grasslands and the forests, they store the water. The people will have to adapt or die. We're working with them to learn what they will have to do. There will be less vegetation, less herding – they will have to find new skills."

"Given that we know all this, Yang Xin, how do you think it is that we can't come up with a better response?" I said.

"The issue is so complicated that it lends itself to standing and looking at it from many different angles. It leads to endless debate because nothing is certain, and so it's easy to avoid action. That's where the world is today – half paralysed by the difficulty of it all. But I think it's up to us. The only thing we have is stories, the stories of those who will be affected.

"Often people say to me, 'But what can I do? I can't be a hard core activist like you!' And I say to them, 'You can do a huge amount. You can practice relaxed environmentalism! It doesn't have to be tense. You'll learn to do it without thinking. Change your light bulbs, travel to work differently, stop wasting food. You can achieve so much with little changes in your daily habits. Then, when enough people do the same, all of a sudden, we'll find we've made an impact.'"

Somehow all the small changes he was advocating seemed rather prosaic, compared to the tidal waves of melt water we could expect in the coming years.

Yet I understood what Yang Xin was doing. He was doing what he could. He was an optimist. He believed in people. He didn't get overwhelmed by the future; he just got on with doing what he could today. For sure, he had a part to play in some of the biggest and toughest challenges of our generation. Telling people some things they'd really rather not know. But he also knew the beauty of small things – one life, one person at a time, one antelope, a single tree in the forest. He knew it because of his relationship with mountains and rivers that had been here for millennia. He saw himself in proportion. He was, and is, a happy soul. He came from loving roots, a carefree boy in the wilds. He'd embarked on a great adventure, had travelled the length of China's mother-river, not out of despair but driven by the sheer joy of life. He'd lost friends on the journey, a huge and heavy price, and from them he'd drawn two powerful lessons. He'd learned to see the whole river – all of life, all of its connections – and he'd learned never to give up.

That was why I'd come to see him.

I was here to remember the see-saw tension between oneness and separateness, between belonging and not, that had held me spell-bound, even as a child. I'd come to say what I knew in my heart: to acknowledge that life is about suffering as well as joy, shame as well as love, and that sometimes there are no adequate answers, sometimes even no answers at all. What matters is how we respond, the choices we make.

I thought about some of the invisible giants I'd come across on the way. I remembered Shakeela and Taddy, Abdullah, Peter and Anwari. They were just a small handful out of the millions, perhaps billions, of invisible giants the world over.

I'd come to stand on the world's rooftop and look out at the future with the same sense of possibility I'd always known deep down, but had sometimes lost in the rush. I wanted to look at my life and my work, unvarnished, and to understand my next step.

~

And so I ask myself, what has this quest of mine really been about? It's been a quest born of intuition. A growing curiosity and awakening to the invisible thread that joins us in a fluid, ever-changing way, across time. A deepening appreciation that each of us is a small but intrinsic part of something much bigger than any of its elements. That if we step back and really look, we see not the individual parts and the seams that separate them, but a powerful, integral whole. In many ways this is a story about learning to see how we all belong.

Sometimes it's been painful. There have been many days when I've let myself down, times when I've missed the point or failed to bridge the gap, situations where I've known in my bones that this really isn't right.

"I've come to see that I'll strangle the ideas I most care about if I hold them so hard, push on them so relentlessly," a friend said to me at the end of a Quest together.

Like her, I'm still learning to hold lightly that which I most cherish. I too fear going unheard – or leaving someone else unheard – our voices carried off in the wind, and our effort spent in vain.

This has also been a quest about choices, practical responses, and the way people work together. Exploring the impact of business on society, the contribution its leaders can make if they decide to do so. It's been about testing the limits of self-interest to define a greater good; respecting how different the same problem or the same opportunity looks from another person's vantage point.

Today, I look at what I've learned from people like Yang Xin and reflect on the road ahead. I'm inspired by the optimism, the mix of pragmatism and hope. I want to keep asking tough questions, to keep looking for answers together with others. I want to celebrate the best we humans have to offer, the grace and compassion I see in so many people. I want to share our stories. For we choose our path in life, whatever circumstance we come from. Each of us chooses how to show up. And we all need leaders of every colour, culture and creed who can stand in the face of difficulty or deprivation and see, not misery, but possibility.

"There will always be another mountain, Lindsay. You have to have an inner smile," Naidu had said to me, as we sat in the garden in Bangalore.

And, yes, I realise, I have begun to smile at who I am. To look straight into my own drive for perfection and see with a bump that it, too, is vanity. Slowly, I've begun to learn some things that matter.

I've learned that there's a brutal beauty in the world that defies interpretation, and that when I let myself go and immerse myself in it, even for a moment, I come to know cohesion and connection. I've learned that what I see in others I also have in me, that the things that make me frail are every bit as much a part of me as those that make me strong. I've learned that I can love others only if I also love myself. I've found that, sometimes, I can tumble backwards in the sea, look up at the sky and float, not sink. I can let my body flow with the swell of each new wave, taste the salt cool in my mouth and feel the breeze upon my face. I can see the sun with my eyes closed and hear the metal sing of bubbles popping in my ears, tiny fern-like funnels that echo with the deep sonic ache of the ocean. And then, when I don't try too hard, I know the whole history of the universe and all the tiny fragments in it are held here in the ocean - and I'm deeply thankful for it.

Footnote:

Shakeela, whom I first met in 2008 on the streets of Delhi, shortly after she had lost her leg in a road accident, and whose story helped energise me to write this book, died in March 2012.

I learned the news in an email from Sanjay which read as follows: "Shakeela has passed away some three weeks back. She was suffering from a chest infection and complications from her wound which had never really healed properly. But put simply, she has died of acute poverty."

Acknowledgements

My deepest debt is to the people who make up the Leaders' Quest community: those who have hosted us in homes, offices and villages all over the world; the participants who have said "yes", trusted us with their time and energy, and come on a Quest; the fellows and mentors whose work has been a consistent source of joy and inspiration; the supporters, donors and trustees whose commitment has made the fellowship programme, and all that it has catalysed, possible.

I would like to thank everyone who has supported our Foundation in different ways – every contribution counts. In particular, I want to thank Chris and Clare Mathias, Paul and Sarah Gay Fletcher, Trixie and Stephen Brenninkmeijer, Andy Hinton, Alastair Gibbons, Ian Fisher, Alan Lewis, Tim Sanderson, Gopal Jain and David Weekley. I am also grateful to the leaders of businesses and institutions who have taken the risk of inviting us to help them and their colleagues to see the world anew. Many people have made this work possible – far more than I can name here. They include Antony Jenkins, Steven Tallman, Jim Hagemann Snabe, Matthew Wright, Grant Gordon, Zia Khan, William Jackson and Virginie Helias.

Several people believed in this project long before I did. Ron Beller challenged me to write this book on an overnight flight back from Delhi; Gene Early is a lifetime friend and teacher and the best person I know at getting to the heart of what really matters; Kemp Battle read the first manuscript and encouraged me to continue. Thank you to Barbara Turner-Vesselago for her invaluable mentoring and for helping me to discover whatever writing skills I might possess. Thank you to my colleague Max Metcalfe for his energy and humour and for ensuring I stayed the course, and to Melanie George and Richard Roberts for making sure I arrived at a conclusion. Anne Wade and Araminta Whitley have both been smart, perceptive readers. Louise V Smith has been a diligent critic and collaborator who has greatly improved this manuscript. I was blessed to find Vala as publishers – its ethos has been a breath of fresh air. I am particularly grateful to Sarah Bird, Vala's CEO, who took the book under her wing and brought it to life, and to my editor, Fi Radford whose intuitive, compassionate feedback proved a turning point in deciding what I had to let go of, as well as what I had to give.

Special appreciation goes to my family. I thank Zac, Joe and Louis for their generosity as sons, their enthusiasm for life, and for the values I see in them every day, which give me hope for the future. Above all I thank my husband David, for his wisdom, tolerance and love. Without it, neither Leaders' Quest nor *Invisible Giants* would exist.

Finally, I owe a huge debt of gratitude to all of my colleagues and partners, past and present, at Leaders' Quest and CORO. Our achievements so far have been a collective effort, made possible by the contributions of a wide circle of people. They have joined me on my journey to see, and make, the connections, and I thank them all for their optimism, passion and hard work.

Many people have helped design and lead Quests and fellowships over time – whether as long-time colleagues, associates or interns. I would like to thank each of them for the part they have played.

Aditi Thorat
Alina Lebedeva
Alison Daly
Amanda Manuel
Amita Jadhav
Amy Barklam
Anna Finn
Anne Wade
Aparna Balakrishnan
Asha Nagre
Beatrice Bauer
Bettina Gherke
Biney Koul
Brijesh Chalise
Cao Zhen
Carolyn Maddox
Catherine Blampied
Charles Anderson
Chen Xin
Chris Harrison
Chris Underhill
Christian Smyth
Clara Thompson
Daniel Lobo
David Levin
Diane Richards
D.M. Naidu
Elaine Sun
Ella Fletcher
Ellen Power
Eric Levine
Ethan Sutaria
Fei Xiaojing
Fiammetta Mancini
Fields Wicker-Miurin
Flavia Temochko
Flavio Stadnik
Gene Early
Gerry Sanseviero
Giles Goodhead
Gitika Mohta
Gopal Jain
Hannah Hopkins
Hannah Lloyd
Hannah Mills
Herman Spruit
Hilary O'Neill
Jackie Hawkins
Jade Phillips
James Wright
Jason Brooks
Jay Shah
Jayma Pau
Jeanne-Marie Gescher
Jennifer Greenway

Jeroen Drontmann
Jessie Finch
Jim Byrne
John Williams
Jon Carr
Jon Huggett
Jos Shoenmaker
Julia Mart
Julie Moy
Kalpana Kar
Kalpana Tribhuvan
Kalyan Tanksale
Kate Duder
Kathryn Hodnett
Kaumudi Karangutkar
Kemp Battle
Kenzie Kwong
Kirsten Rudolph
Lakshapathi Pendyala
Lewis Husain
Liz Lowther
Loïc Sadoulet
Louise Smith
Lu Yao
Mac (Tim) Macartney
Mahendra Rokade
Mani Kalliath
Marian Goodman
Mark Norbury
Marta Garcia Abadia
Mary Elizabeth Walters
Mary Macleod
Matthew Little
Max Metcalfe
Melanie George
Melanie Katzman
Michael Melcher
Molly Loyd
Natasha Parekh
Nigel Topping
Nutan Bhagat
Pan Jiaen
Paula Ho
Pauline Elliot
Phiona Cipriani
Pia Petersson
Pradeep Kar
Pramod Walande
Rahul Gaikwad
Rahul Gaware
Ram Shelke
Renee Lau
Richard Roberts
Richard Wong
Rosanda McGrath

Rose Ogden
Rosemary Brown
Rowan Belchers
Ryan Chapman
Sameer Shaikh
Sandhya Sardar
Sasha Rodricks
Sayo Ayodele
Sayyed Ibrahim Kadri
Shishir Sawant
Shrikant Naik
Sidhharth Kharat
Simon Hampel
Sophie Bray
Sophie Pinder
Steven Tallman
Subi Rangan
Sudhir Salve
Sue Cheshire
Sujata Khandekar
Sujatha Gopi
Supriya Sonar
Suresh Kumar
Suryakant Kamble
Suzanne Gowler
Tang Haisong
Tom Wright
Tu Bin
Ulrich Nettesheim
Vaishnavi Adhav
Veena H.G.
Veronique Van Theemsche
Vijay Dethe
Vilas Sarmalkar
Vinay Rao
Vincenzo Perrone
Vishwajit Singh
Wendy Luhabe
William Prinsloo
Wu Shan
Yang Yang
Yang Yuzhu
Yvonne Corpuz
Zhanna Veyts
Zhang Fan
Zhang Lanying
Zheng Lin Lin

References

1. Viktor E Frankl, *Man's Search for Meaning*, Boston: Beacon Press, 2006.
2. Brené Brown, *The Power of Vulnerability*, talk delivered at TEDxHouston in June 2010. Available at http://www.ted.com/talks/brene_brown_on_vulnerability.html.
3. Adam Kahane, *Power and Love: A Theory and Practice of Social Change*, San Francisco: Berrett-Koehler Publishers, 2010.

About Vala

Vala is an adventure
in community supported publishing.

We are a co-operative
bringing books to the world that explore and celebrate
the human spirit with brave and authentic
ways of thinking and being.

Books that seek to help us find our own meanings
that may lead us in new and *unexpected* directions.

Vala's co-operative members
- suggest authors
- design
- write
- support the writing process
- get together for book-making evenings
- promote and sell Vala books through their own networks.

Members come together to celebrate and launch each
new publication. Together we decide what happens to any
profit that we make.

Vala exists to bring us all into fuller relationship with our
world, ourselves, and each other.

To find out more visit us at *www.valapublishers.coop*

 Vala